I0805943

SUFI CUISINE

NEVIN HALICI

SUFI CUISINE

Translated by
ÜMIT HUSSEIN

Foreword by
CLAUDIA RODEN

Original Miniatures by
AHMET EFE

SAQI

Translator's Note

I am greatly indebted to the following websites which were an enormous help throughout the translation of this book:
'Serving the Guest: A Sufi Cookbook & Art Gallery' and 'A Mevlevi Glossary' (www.dar-al-masnavi.org/mevlevi-glossary.html).

SAQI BOOKS
Gable House, 18-24 Turnham Green Terrace
London W4 1QP
www.saqibooks.com

First published by Saqi Books 2005
This paperback edition published 2024

ISBN 9780863568367
eISBN 9780863568220
A full CIP record for this book is available from the British Library.

Printed and bound by Printworks Global Ltd, London/Hong Kong.

To the beloved memory of my father, Sabri Halıcı,
and my mother, Hanım Halıcı.

In short my whole life can be summed up with these words:
I was raw, I was cooked, I was burned.

DIVAN-I KEBIR 5: 69-COUPLET:815

'When it shines, approach the radiance where God is manifest; in its light the full moon seems as a loaf, and the sun like the baker who cooks it.'

IBID., 5:487-COUPLET:6689

'Think of the heavens and the earth as an apple grown
on God's omnipotent tree.'

MESNEVI BOOK 4: P. 267-COUPLET:1869

'The heart, the eyes, the stomach feed on light,
because the origin of food is heavenly light.'

DIVAN-I KEBIR 5: 193-VERSE:2218

Contents

Abbreviations used

c	couplet
d	Divan-ı Kebir
fm	Fihi Maafih
g	gram
kg	kilogram
m	Mesnevi
mek	Mektubat
tsp	teaspoon
dsp	dessertspoon
tbsp	tablespoon

Information about quotes

M6:7-C:19 means Mesnevi, book 6, page 7, 19th couplet.

FOREWORD

by Claudia Roden

In all the years that I have been researching food around the world I have never come across anyone as passionately committed to recovering and upholding the culinary heritage of their country as Nevin Halıcı. I met her more than twenty years ago when chance took me to Konya in Central Anatolia, a religious and traditional city inland, in central Turkey, where women wear long dresses and scarves over their heads and men go out alone without their wives. I was there to attend a symposium on Turkish food and a cooking competition between local villages. Both events had been organised by the Halıcı family (there are three brothers and two sisters) who owned a carpet shop and who were also in charge of the Culture and Tourism Association. Nevin's brother

Feyzi Halıcı made Konya a centre of folk and popular culture. A poet and one-time senator, he instigated the Mevlana festival of Whirling Dervishes, troubadour and rose festivals, jereed horse races, pigeon racing competitions, the national javelin games, folk poetry, music, and Koranic reading competitions. With his sister he made Konya a centre for gastronomic revival.

Elated by the events, I asked the family if they would consider doing an international food symposium. A few months later I received a letter asking for a list of people who might be interested in attending a gastronomic congress, the first of many that ran biannually until 1996. It turned out to be the most fantastic, magical event. Starting with a stay at the Pera Palas in Istanbul, we were invited to travel to several cities and to taste all manner of delicious regional foods, many of which were unknown even to the Turkish gastronomes travelling with us. We heard scholarly lectures about the history of Turkish food; we visited palace kitchens and local bazaars and went to see artisans at work. We went to regional restaurants and were invited to people's homes and even a factory where the workers brought their dishes from home for a banquet. We were also entertained by belly dancers, sword dancers and whirling dervishes. A highlight was when several sheep were cooked in a hole in a wrought iron-worker's garden.

Nevin is the most respected food writer in Turkey. She has made the first extensive study of their regional foods, recording recipes, the occasions on which dishes are served, the way of life of which they form part, and their significance. She went from village to village, knocking on doors, watching women cook, attending their traditional get-togethers. She taught cooking in a girl's school in Izmir and was asked to demonstrate to chefs in some of the big hotels where the management wanted to introduce regional dishes. (Most of the cooks of Turkey are trained in the classic Istanbul style and regional foods are unknown to them.) She is the very best guide to the delicacies of Turkey. We have tramped together from tripe soup and pie specialist, fish restaurant and kebab house to pastry and milk pudding maker.

Sufi Cuisine has been long in the making and is close to Nevin's heart. It is nothing like an ordinary cookery book. It has opened for me a world I never knew existed, the world of the thirteenth-century Muslim Sufi mystic and poet Mevlana Jalal al Din Rumi, founder of the Mevlevi Order of the Whirling Dervishes. In it we discover the intimate workings of the Order – their codes, initiation rituals, daily life – which turn very much around the kitchen and the table. Rumi's poetry is imbued with culinary metaphor and imagery. Nevin has collected his verses where there are references to food and wine, cooking and eating as well as the recipes for the foods he mentions and the dishes he describes. She has also included dishes from later in the Mevlevi tradition – some from the nineteenth-century cookery book by the dervish Eşref Dede, and others that are still current today in Konya, which was Mevlana's home, and where Nevin lives.

They reveal the sensuous quality, the tastes and smells and feel of thirteenth-century Konya, when the city was the capital of the Seljuk sultanate which controlled most of Anatolia. It was, then, a centre of brilliant culture that attracted scholars, poets, artists and mystics from all over the Islamic world. The highly sophisticated gastronomy that developed there was influenced by Persian cooking because the Seljuks also ruled Isfahan. It was absorbed later on into Ottoman cuisine because palace cooks in Constantinople and those in the Janissaries followed the Sufi order. Some of the classic Turkish cuisine we know today is a legacy from the Seljuk period. For those interested in the history of food, therefore, *Sufi Cuisine* also illuminates the development of Turkish and Middle Eastern cookery.

This book has many facets – it is a cultural history, a book of poetry, a culinary memoir and a collection of recipes. It also gives a rare insight into the spiritual wisdom and philosophy that Rumi expressed through ecstatic love poetry seeking to unite humanity in love, respect and brotherhood. It is a timely and welcome publication in that it represents to us a tolerant, peaceful, loving face of Islam.

Claudia Roden
March 2005

PREFACE

'Farewell to you, but this is not the farewell of a departing one;
Such farewells are echoed again and again.'

MEK:49

From the thirteenth century to the present day the works of the great Mevlana, one of humanity's prodigies, have provided endless insight into the world of inner meaning.

Mevlana is the *pir* or founder of the Mevlevi order. He reveals that the route to God is via the Shari'a (Islamic law) and the Sufi path. The Shari'a is the division of fundamental rules and ideas accepting God as the source of Islam. The tariqat (Sufi path) is the spiritual path following the belief that Islamic mysticism (tasavvuf) leads directly to an understanding of God. Every tariqat has its own observances and rules of conduct. In the ninth and tenth centuries 'tariqat' was used to refer to the spiritual path followed by every Sufi mystic.

The tariqat that first came into existence in the circles of the Sufi mystic guides, known as sheikhs, when they began to meet from the twelfth century, originally aimed to set out the guidelines for worship and life to the sheikhs' disciples. In time the name came to identify a community of disciples, under the leadership of a sheikh, whose lives and way of worshipping were governed by specific rules. A mutasavvıf, or Sufi, is someone who has chosen to live his life according to the tasavvuf. There are numerous tariqats in Islam, such as the Mevlevi Order, the Qadiri Order, and the Naqshbandi tariqat. Every tariqat member is a Sufi, obliged to obey the rules of his own tariqat. The cuisine presented in this book as Sufi cuisine is, in fact, the cuisine of the Mevlevi Order.

To express his ideas that were in every respect so inspirational, Mevlana used various symbols, one of which was food. By saying 'My life can be summed up with the words "I was raw, I was cooked, I was burned"' he used food terminology to illustrate his most significant philosophy of life. He was, moreover, a source of endless information on practically every subject related to food, such as agriculture, medicine, aesthetics, flavour, table setting, entertaining, teamwork and cooking; he also left behind several recipes. In this way the eminent Mevlana made us a gift of the food culture of his era, in the form of a very informative and highly significant archive. There are several factors pointing to the high status of cuisine in that period. Firstly, written rules regarding the organisation of the kitchen and its working came into being in the thirteenth century; secondly, a memorial tombstone for Mevlana's famous cook, Ateş-bazı Veli, was erected after his death, and thirdly, it is a fact that a dervish's training begins in the kitchen.

The fact that many of the dishes mentioned by Mevlana still exist in Konya today inspired me to write this book. Being a Konya native definitely helped, as certain dishes Mevlana refers to in his works, like tutmaç (pastry dough cut into squares and cooked with meat and yogurt), bulamaç (sweet, buttery soup), sirkencübin (honey mixed with vinegar) and quince stewed with pekmez (grape molasses), are unfamiliar not only to people outside the region, but also to the younger generation in Konya. This book sets out to present the cuisine of the Mevlevi Order, referring to written and spoken sources, as well as to the cuisine passed down to Konya through the Seljuks (May God rest the souls of the great Mevlana, Şems-i Tebriz, Sultan Veled and Ahmet Eflaki, whose works have shed light on Mevlana's era, and of the Esteemed Abdülbaki Gölpınarlı, whose translations gave me access to these authors). While asking God to rest the souls of all the deceased writers whose works helped me, I would like to wish good health to all those who are still alive. I am eternally grateful to my elder brother, Feyzi Halıcı, who played the biggest part in making this book become a reality, and to my family. My thanks also to Professor Dr Nilgün Çelebi, for her assistance in all matters, Ayla Halıcı, for her assistance in historical matters, to Metin, Nermin and Hasan Halıcı for their endless support, and to Ümit Hussein, for translating the book. I should like to give separate thanks to my very dear friends Claudia Roden and Jill Norman who helped with the publication of the book and were constantly by my side offering support. My sincere thanks also to Ahmet Efe for the excellent miniatures he has contributed to this work, and to Gülnur and John McMillan, who were by my side from the beginning of this project to the end. I also thank Ms Sarah al-Hamad and Dr Penny Warburton of Saqi Books for publishing my book. I am greatly indebted to the sources who lit the path and made this book a reality, my panellist friends, and everyone else whose efforts contributed to its creation.

Nevin Halıcı
14 June 2003

INTRODUCTION

In the thirteenth century Mevlana founded a philosophy that aimed to unite people in love, respect and tolerance. From Konya he transmitted messages of love, friendship and brotherhood to the people of his war-ravaged era. While they aimed to explain the most exalted points of Sufism on the one hand, his works were also written in a style that could educate ordinary people – he talked about all aspects of everyday life, using stories and jokes to make them universally accessible. Mevlana often referred to food to explain his elevated ideas; he as good as put together the culinary archive of his era, in addition to passing on a few dishes to us.

The fact that a Sufi's initiation begins in the kitchen, that there are several written regulations regarding the organisation of the kitchen, that these regulations refer to the teamwork in operation there, and that a memorial tomb was built for a cook shows how highly cuisine was regarded in Anatolia in the thirteenth century. Another of the special attributes of Mevlevi cuisine, already famous for these characteristics, is that it is one of the principal roots of Turkish cuisine. It will also be seen from this study that the cuisine served in dervish lodges was more refined than folk cuisine. This book sets out to present Mevlevi cuisine, backed up by written and spoken references. To this end I first of all studied Mevlana's complete works. Secondly, I leafed through other important works that throw light on that era, such as Şems-i Tebriz's *Makalat* (Conversations), Sultan Veled's *İbtidaname* and Eflaki's *Tales of the Wise*, and to gather information about food.

Part one of the book contains key information about the Mevlevi Order and Islamic mysticism (tasavvuf), Mevlana's life and his philososphy. Part two contains food-related couplets from Mevlana's works and part three contains the recipes found in Mevlana's works, the dishes he refers to that still exist in Konya, the dishes in the *Tales of the Wise* and other sources connected with the Mevlevi Order, and recipes taken from Ali Eşref Dede's *Treatise on Cuisine*, a work from the Edirne Mevlevi division.

A Brief History of Mevlana's Life

Mevlana Jalaluddin al-Rumi was born on 30 September 1207 in Balkh, in the north of Afghanistan. His real name was Muhammed Jalaluddin. Hudavendigar, (Lord) Mevlana and Rumi (Anatolia) were titles bestowed on him later.

His family is said to be descended from Hazreti Ali on his mother's side and from the Caliph Abubakr on his father's side. Both his mother and father came from eminent families in Balkh. His paternal grandmother was Melike-i Cihan Emanullah Sultan, daughter of the Horasan Sultan Jalaluddin Harzemşah. His mother was Mümine Hatun, daughter of the Balkh Chief

Rükneddin. His father, Muhammed Bahaeddin Veled, like his grandfather before him, was a renowned scholar.

Born in 1148, Bahaeddin Veled lost his father at the age of two and was brought up in the Horasan palace by his highly cultured mother. Despite being a Sultan's son he devoted himself to religion rather than government and politics and became one of the most celebrated scholars of his era. According to Eflaki, the acclaimed historian of the time, Bahaeddin Veled became such a sage that in one night three hundred of the most eminent learned and religious men of the era dreamed that the Prophet Muhammad gave him the title Sultan'ul Ulema, Sultan of Scholars, and from that day on Mevlana's father went under that title. Sultan'ul Ulema used his extensive knowledge and faith in God to give lessons and sermons in Balkh, where he was deeply respected by his large following of disciples and ordinary people.

However, the fact that he did not share the logical beliefs originating from Greek philosophy held by certain learned men resulted in a disagreement between him and Fakhreddin Razi, one of the philosophers of the era who did subscribe to those views. When Sultan Aladdin Muhammed Harzemşah sided with Razi, Sultan'ul Ulema decided to emigrate. The threat of Mongol invasion also played an important role in this decision, and between 1212 and 1213 Bahaeddin Veled was on the road, with his family and closest friends. Shortly afterwards the Mongols invaded the city and razed it to the ground.

This journey, which started when Mevlana was between five and six years old, included Baghdad, Kufa, Mecca, Damascus, Malatya, Erzincan and Akşehir, and ended at Karaman, then called Larende. Bahaeddin Veled continued his teachings here.

In 1226 in Karaman, at the age of eighteen, Mevlana married Gevher Hatun, the daughter of Hodja Şerafeddin Lala, who emigrated with them from Balkh. They had two sons from this marriage, Sultan Veled and Ala'addin. Years later Gevher Hatun died; from his second marriage, to Kerra Hatun, Mevlana had two sons, Muzaffereddin and Emir Alim Çelebi, and a daughter, Melike Hatun.

Sultan Aladdin Keykubad I invited Bahaeddin Veled to Konya. On 3 May 1228 Bahaeddin Veled arrived at the capital, Konya, which was to be his final stop, with his family and closest friends. The Sultan and the townsfolk greeted them as they entered. The Sultan invited Sultan Bahaeddin Veled to stay at the palace, but Bahaeddin Veled said the madrasah (a theological school attached to a mosque) was more appropriate for someone on the path to knowledge, and they settled at the Altunapa Madrasah. Here Bahaeddin Veled continued with his teachings, surrounding himself with new disciples, headed by Sultan Aladdin Keykubad. Bahaeddin Veled died on 24 February 1231.

Following the loss of his father, Mevlana's life can be considered in terms of four phases of development: preparation, ecstasy, tranquillity and maturity.

The Phase of Preparation

Mevlana received his early education from his father. He devoted his time exclusively to the study of divine knowledge and became mature while still a small child, acquiring the ability to reason. Following the death of his father, one of Bahaeddin Veled's disciples, Seyid Burhaneddin Muhakkik-i Tırmizi, came to Konya from Kayseri, took up Mevlana's spiritual education from where his father had left off and completed it. They went to Aleppo together, where Mevlana received instruction from Kemaleddin-İbn Al-Adim. Mevlana later went to Damascus, where he also spent a long time; there he met Arabi, Hamevi, Kirmani, Konevi and other scholars who extended his knowledge.

When he returned to Konya from Damascus Seyyid Burhaneddin put him through three forty-day *çiles* – periods of retirement and fasting, without allowing him to leave his cell even once. During this period Mevlana devoted himself exclusively to worship and contemplation and emerged with a purified mind, having attained a maturity that opened him up to divine secrets. Seeing that his education was now complete, Seyyid Burhaneddin informed Mevlana of his wish to return to Kayseri. When Mevlana, deeply grieved, asked the reason why, Seyyid Burhaneddin replied, 'You are now a gentle and tolerant sage, matured with all the knowledge pertaining to this world and the next, at the peak of perfection. You lack nothing now. I'm leaving, but after me you will have a companion so exceptional that you will complete each other. After this, my son, your writings and words will put fresh strength in people's souls, you will flood the world of knowledge with God's compassion. The living dead in this world will come back to life in the realm of love and meaning you will show them.' So saying, he returned to Kayseri.

The Phase of Ecstasy

While Mevlana, one of the foremost scholars of his era, was devoting his time in Konya to teaching students and enlightening the people, the fiery Şems-i Tebrizi, whom Seyyid Burhaneddin had singled out, and who would inflame Mevlana and complete him, arrived in Konya on 29 November 1244. Şems was a dervish who roamed from country to country in search of a murshid (spiritual guide) to complete the gaps he believed existed in his spiritual knowledge.

When they met Mevlana gave such profound answers to his questions that Şems fell to the ground unconscious, and thus began their friendship. The two sages withdrew to deepen their understanding of God's radiance with *sohbet* – spiritual discussions. Together they experienced a phase in which they reached the highest peak of ecstasy and rapture. Mevlana abandoned his teachings and sermons. But hostility on the part of the townsfolk, envious of this friendship, resulted in Şems going to Damascus. Devastated by the separation, Mevlana went into seclusion, refusing to see anyone. The townsfolk repented. After the arrival of a letter from Şems the townsfolk sent Mevlana's son Sultan Veled to Damascus, with one of Mevlana's poems. Following this invitation Şems returned to Konya.

The two sages resumed their spiritual debates, but envy raised its head again and on the night of 5 December 1247, Şems suddenly disappeared. He had been dispatched by malevolent followers, but Mevlana was not informed. Mevlana went to Damascus to look for Şems, but in vain. Interpreting the situation from a spiritual point of view, he returned to Konya. The poems expressing the pain of this separation are to be found in the *Divan-ı Kebir*.

The Phase of Tranquillity

Following his phase of ecstasy with Şems, Mevlana's union with Selahaddin Zerkubi, formed when he was at the highest peak of enlightenment and understanding, is known as the Phase of Tranquillity. Sultan Veled illustrates in a ghazal, included in his *İbtidaname*, what Mevlana found in Şems and Selahaddin: 'Why did we sleep? That man we call Şemseddin has returned. To display his beauty, to parade in search of adventure he has changed his clothes and reappeared. Is not the wine of life you drink from a glass the same wine when poured into a bowl? What is different?'

The friendship between Selahaddin and Mevlana, who found Şems' light in Selahaddin, lasted for ten years. Selahaddin died in January 1259.

The Phase of Maturity

Following the phase that began with Şems, in which he reached the highest point of ecstasy and rapture, the phase of Mevlana's life that he spent with Selahaddin was the phase of tranquillity which blossomed out of the state of perfect enlightenment and discernment.

The phase that was to follow was the mature phase of 'Perfection', which Mevlana expressed as 'I was raw, I was cooked, I was burned.' During this period Çelebi Hüsameddin played an important role in Mevlana's life. After the death of Selahaddin, Mevlana's close friend and officially named successor Hüsameddin, told Mevlana that he needed to write an inspirational, educative work worthy of his perfection. Mevlana had had the same thought. Now he took a piece of paper from the folds of his turban, on which were written the first eighteen couplets of the *Mesnevi*, saying to Hüsameddin, 'If you write, I'll recite.' Thus began the *Mesnevi*. Hüsameddin remained constantly by Mevlana's side until the work was completed, while sitting, walking along the road, during the sema, even when he was in the hamam. Mevlana recited and Husameddin wrote.

The *Mesnevi* is a work that has made people say of Mevlana, 'He is not a prophet, but he has a book.'

Mevlana's Death

In the winter of 1273 Mevlana suddenly fell ill and was confined to his bed. On 17 December he attained the moment of reunion with his beloved that he had longed for throughout his life:

> When it is you who takes life, death tastes like sugar:
> As long as I am with you dying tastes sweeter to me than sweet life. DI:308-C:2854

For Mevlana the day of his death was a day of celebration which would reunite him with God. The moment of his death is regarded as the moment when he is reunited with his beloved, and referred to as 'Şeb-i Arus', the wedding night. It has been celebrated by Mevlevi Sufis as a joyful event, in the form of helva gatherings, from the time of his death up to the present time.

Mevlana, who requested that there should be no mourning after his death, said:

After our death do not look for my grave in the ground,
My grave is in the hearts of the wise.

Mevlana's tomb, completed in 1274 in Konya, was designed by the architect Tebrizli Bedreddin. The following Persian couplet by Mullah Cami is inscribed on the door of the tomb:

This place has become a lovers' Kaaba.
He who came here unfinished has been completed.

Mevlana's Works

Mevlana wrote the *Mesnevi, Divan-ı Kebir, Fih Mafih, Mecalis Seb'a* and *Mektubat* (Letters).

The Seven Selected Recommendations from Mevlana's works are:

Be like the sun in compassion and mercy.
In hiding others' defects and faults be like the night.
In anger and irritation be like the dead.
Be like flowing water in generosity and offering help.
In tolerance be like the ocean.
Be like the earth in humility and humbleness.
Either seem as you are or be as you seem.

Mevlana's Philosophy of Life

As shown earlier, Mevlana was the founder of a movement uniting people in the crucible of love, respect and tolerance. According to Eflaki, Mevlana was a man of refined, sound common sense, whose witty remarks and combination of worldly and spiritual knowledge in the face of daily occurrences spread happiness to those around him. He was serious in the company of influential people, humble when he was with the poor. Mevlana, inclined by nature to embrace every living being with love and compassion, particularly the weak, said, 'Anyone looking for friends without faults shall remain friendless.' His works are full of stories that speak with affection and tolerance of children, women of ill repute, animals and plants.

Mevlana, who set great store by freedom of thought and could not endure narrow-mindedness or unsympathetic behaviour, guided people towards goodness with his inspirational views and faith. He advocated the need to look ahead at all times and leave yesterday in the past. One day during the sema, when he had reached a state of ecstasy, a drunk entered and threw the place into confusion. When the other Sufis were hostile to the man, Mevlana reproached them by saying, 'He's the one who drank wine, you are the ones behaving like dissolute drunks.'

For his tolerance of other religions Mevlana was loved and respected not only by those of his own faith but also by those from other religious communities in Anatolia at that time. At his funeral all the people of Anatolia, including Christians and Jews, walked side by side with Muslims, all following their own customs, reading verses from the Book of Psalms, the Torah, the New Testament and the Koran. Unable to maintain order during the ceremony, the officials informed the Sultan, who summoned the leaders of the other religions and asked, 'What has this event to do with you?' 'Mevlana is our King,' they replied. 'Just as you see Mevlana as the Muhammad of your era we regard him as the Christ or Moses of our time. If you consider yourselves his *muhib* then we regard ourselves a thousand times more as his slaves and disciples. Mevlana said, "Seventy-two nations hear their secrets from us, we are a nay (reed flute) that makes hundreds of sounds using the same pitch."' A Greek monk said, 'Mevlana is like bread. Have you ever seen anyone hungry run away from bread?' As a result of this, everyone was granted the right to take part in the ceremony and the entire population of Anatolia bade Mevlana farewell as he set out on his final journey.

Islamic Mysticism and the Mevlevi Order

The Sufi path means knowing God and becoming whole with Him (Wahdat al-Wujud). There are two ways of following this path. The first depends on withdrawal from the world, living an ascetic existence and worshipping constantly day and night. The second path seeks the way to God through love and ecstasy. According to this view everything you see in the universe is the manifestation of God. The divine identity within a person's body during his or her lifetime, known as the soul, also yearns continually for reunion with the place it came from: in other words, God. This yearning gives birth to divine love, cultivates it and elevates it to a state of ecstasy. With this love a person matures and learns God's secrets. God is a constant presence in the action of creation, a continually renewed form of complete self control, a light and love. He is present in every kind of expression, explanation and description. God's existence transgresses the boundaries of the human mind and goes beyond the human capacity of comprehension. It is only by filling the heart with divine love that a person will be able to see God through the eyes of a lover. Through this ecstatic love a person gradually reaches the state of perfect maturity. Ecstasy is the highest point of the love and yearning for God. The world, the planets, every creature down to the atomic nucleus whirls in this ecstasy, chanting the name of Allah.

Mevlana chose the second Sufi path, that of love and ecstasy. He used music and the sema, both accepted in Islamic mysticism, as vehicles for exciting love and intensifying the feeling of ecstasy.

The essence of Mevlevi teachings and practices comes from the mystical dimensions of Islam (*tasavvuf*) and Mevlana's vast world of thought. The Mevlevi Order, moulded from Mevlana's philosophy of love, is a large and widespread Sufi order. As time went on, it developed various rules, and took its shape from figurative actions and behaviour. These metaphors demonstrate that taking part in the whirling dance, as well as the music used in the ceremony, are roads leading a person to God.

Literature Related to Sufi Cuisine

The only work on Sufi cuisine written in modern Turkish is the *Food Treatise* of Ali Eşref Dede, the sheikh of the Edirne Mevlevi Dergah. It was published in 1992 by Feyzi Halıcı and is the only work devoted to Mevlevi cuisine, containing select recipes. There are chapters on rich soups, salads and pickles, kebabs, grilled cutlets, desserts, lokma (fried, syrupy dumplings), lalanga and börek, dolma and lamb's trotters, fried börek with pumpkin, köfte, kalye (aubergines with meat and onions) and vegetable stews. It also tells you how to prepare bone marrow and yahnis (lamb stews made with onions and tomatoes), pilavs and hoşafs, and even how to make ice from water! Ali Eşref Dede provides sumptuous recipes for sweets using gold vark and also other spices not found in classic Turkish or Turkish folk cuisine.

One of Mevlana's last descendants, Celaleddin Çelebi, who recently passed away, imparted valuable information about Mevlevi cuisine at an 'International Food Congress'. Other relevant articles and papers include 'Food in Mevlana's *Mesnevi* and *Divan-ı Kebir*,' 'Mevlana's Food Imagery,' 'Mevlana's Food Symbolism' and 'From Planted Grain to Bread in Mevlana's Poetry'.

Organisation and Training in the Kitchen

> That unparalleled beauty has taken possession of my heart's kitchen with all its title deeds; and is smashing my pots, pans, plates, platters to pieces. D4:33-C:264

This couplet demonstrates the existence of an established kitchen in Mevlana's time. The Mevlevi Order that came into being after his death created various written rules concerning the kitchen and the organisation of the work therein. Of all the dervish orders, the Mevlevi Order has the greatest number of regulations regarding customary observances, and is the strictest about obeying them.

The kitchen is the first, sacred place where these rules are put into practice. The kitchens of dergahs are not vastly different in layout from other kitchens, but they have different functions, because a Mevlevi Sufi's training begins there. Anyone wishing to enter the Mevlevi Order must observe the workings of the kitchen for three days from a designated area. There is also an area where new disciples learn to perform the *sema*.

The kitchen is also known as Ateş-baz, in honour of Ateş-baz Veli (Mevlana's cook). The framed inscription 'Oh Holy Ateş-baz Veli' was to be found above every stove in the kitchen. As Celaleddin Çelebi writes, 'If certain misguided individuals who have never been inside a kitchen, but have written about it from hearsay have said that coffee and sherbet were drunk and guests received there, I would like to show that this is contrary to custom. There is a 'Soul' in the kitchen that nobody wishes to disturb. For this reason people only entered the kitchen if it was for something important. They would approach the door in silence, salute with a gesture of the head, gently sound the door knocker, say 'With Your Leave Holy Dervishes, Hu' if the door was open, slowly explain what they desired to the person who answered the door and never enter without the permission of the senior dervish (Dede) on duty, or without being invited in. Once they entered they would carry out their business immediately and then walk out of the door backwards, saluting with their heads.'

In the era before the tariqats were closed down the kitchen was the heart of the Mevlevi lodges. In Konya, the Çelebi (dervish leader) represented the Mevlevi Order, whereas in other dervish lodges it was the sheikh. In Konya, the Tarikatçı Dede, the chief spiritual guide of the Mevlevis, trained the dervishes, whereas in other lodges it was the Aşçı Dede, Chief of the Kitchen and Master of Ceremonies. The Aşçı Dede's responsibility was the supervision of the new disciple wishing to enter the *dergah* who had to pledge his allegiance to the Aşçı Dede after which he was entrusted to the Kazancı Dede, the Keeper of the Cauldron.

The Aşçı Dede was in charge of the kitchen, while the Kazancı Dede, the İçeri Meydancı (the Chief Steward and Master of Ceremonies for inside the *tekke*), the Dishwasher Dede and the Halife Dede (the chief successor), were in charge of running the tekke. The Aşçı Dede organised the budget, ran the tekke and trained the disciples. The Kazancı Dede was his assistant. The Halife Dede instructed the new initiates in the kitchen and taught them Mevlevi ways and rules of conduct. The İçeri Meydancı answered to the sheikh and communicated his orders. These Dedes were known as 'dergah officers'.

Anyone wishing to enter a dervish lodge came with his family's permission and pledged his allegiance to the Aşçı Dede in the latter's presence; if it was accepted he would sit for three days on the *saka postu*, a pelt on a raised platform on the left-hand side of the kitchen entrance, and observe the workings of the kitchen. If he decided to stay he was taken to the Kazancı Dede, whom he informed of his decision.

If the Keeper of the Cauldron approved, the novice had to run errands for eighteen days, dressed in the same outfit he had worn since his arrival. At the end of this period the Kazancı Dede made a request for clothing to the Aşçı Dede who would then send for the kitchen *tennure*, the wide-skirted garment worn by a Mevlevi dervish, which was a little narrower and shorter than the sema tennure, worn while performing the sema, and all the other dervish garb. The young novice would shed his own clothing and put on these garments. This ritual was known as 'undressing' and meant that the initiate was beginning his life as a Sufi. The undressed kitchen novice, called 'nev-niyaz', would then begin a 1001-day trial period of çile in the kitchen under the supervision of the Keeper of the Cauldron.

During the çile period the novice was tested, being forced to repeat the same task over and over again. His obedience and movements were scrutinised, his patience and forbearance measured. If the novice himself decided he could not endure these tests he 'broke the çile' and left the dergah. If it was the Dedes who decided he was unsuitable, the toes of his shoes were turned towards the door, signifying that he had to leave. If he had to leave because of misconduct, he was sent on his way via the 'door of insolence' situated at the back of the *tekke*.

The Mevlevi Order, established after the death of Mevlana, set up certain rules regarding table manners and the organisation of work in the kitchen, some of which have survived to the present day. Gölpınarlı, who set out the first known regulations for the organisation of work, in both Konya and Turkish cuisine, outlines the eighteen kitchen duties as follows:

1. Kazanci Dede (Keeper of the Cauldron and Master of Service) was a sheikh and spent the mornings in the kitchen. He was in charge of all matters concerning the kitchen and was the Aşçı Dede's deputy.
2. Halife Dede trained and instructed the novices recently admitted to the kitchen.
3. Dışarı Meydancı (Master of External Housework) informed the dervishes in retreat of the sheikh's or Aşçı Dede's orders.
4. The Launderer was responsible for organising the laundry.
5. The Latrine Cleaner was responsible for organising the cleaning of the latrines, the fountain used for ablutions and

the washbasins.

6. The Sherbet Maker made sherbet and served it to guests.
7. The Dishwasher organised the washing-up.
8. The Master of the Cupboard was in charge of the cleaning of cupboards and utensils and carried out the duties of a tinsmith.
9. The Purchaser of Provisions went to the market in the mornings with his baskets and bought food.
10. Somatçı (Tablesetter) laid and cleared the table.
11. İçeri Meydancısı (Master of Internal Housework) made and served coffee to the novices, and to the dedes when they visited the kitchen on Fridays.
12. İçeri Kandilcisi (Keeper of the Internal Oil Lamps) cleaned and lit the oil lamps in the kitchen.
13. Tahmisçi (Coffee Grinder) ground the coffee.
14. The Bedmaker made up the beds and folded them away.
15. Dışarı Kandilcisi (Keeper of the External Oil Lamps) lit the oil lamps outside the dergah.
16. The Sweeper was responsible for sweeping the garden and surrounding area.
17. The Keeper of Candlesticks was responsible for the maintenance of the candlesticks in the kitchen.
18. The Footman ran errands, fetched and carried, and performed menial tasks. A novice admitted into the kitchen started off as a footman. If there were fewer than eighteen novices in the kitchen, one novice would have to carry out several duties.If there were more, they were each allotted individual responsibilities.

In his paper 'International Food Congress', Celaleddin Çelebi outlines these duties slightly differently; the eighteen duties in the 'Matbah Şerif' (Sacred Kitchen), are:

1. To serve the Aşçı Dede (General Director), who was the absolute master of the Matbah Şerif, occupying the position of Ateş-baz Veli, whose spiritual representative he was.
2. To serve the Kazancı Dede, Keeper of the Cauldron (General Director's Deputy), Aşçı Dede's principal assistant.
3. To serve the Halife Dede (Chief of Religious Matters).
4. To serve the İçeri Meydancı Dede, Master of Internal Housework (Chief of Matters of Discipline).
5. Cooking.
6. Purchaser of Provisions (responsible for purchasing food).
7. Pantry Stores Keeper.
8. Dish Washer.
9. The Master of the Cupboard (the disciple who carries out a tinsmith's duties, was responsible for the maintenance and putting away of saucepans, cauldrons, pots and pans).
10. The Stove Kindler brought in the fuel from the store outside the kitchen and kindled the stove, saying, 'Bismillahirahmanirrahim'.
11. The Sweeper.
12. The Footman performed the first duties of a novice, errands involving fetching and carrying on foot.
13. The Bed Maker made up and folded away the beds when, for reasons of overcrowding or for any other reason, the disciples had to sleep in the kitchen.
14. Tahmisçi, the Coffee Grinder, roasted the coffee for the Meydan, the large section of the Mevlevi lodge where

religious ceremonies were performed, and for the Dedes.

15. The Keeper of the Oil Lamps cleaned the candlesticks and oil lamps and lit them.
16. Somatçı, the Tablesetter, set and served at the table and poured the water.
17. The Gardener looked after the flower garden and the fruit and vegetable plots.
18. The Cleaner of latrines cleaned the fountains used for ablutions, the washbasins and latrines. This was the final duty assigned to a disciple before he was promoted to the position of Dede, and was designed to test his forbearance.

The First Great Sufi Chef and Chef of Turkish Cuisine

> The water should be boiled and the chef skilled, that the soup in the pot may cook without spilling. M5: 239-B:1380

In Mevlana's time a chef's profession carried high status. The respect shown to Ateş-baz Veli ('He who plays with fire') demonstrates this fact. He is probably the world's first chef to have had a memorial tomb built in his honour, and it is located in Meram, Konya. It is constructed with flame-coloured stones. The inscription on the façade reads: 'This tomb is the grave of the son of İzzet, the celebrated Muslim who gave his life for Islam, Şems Yusuf Ateş-baz. He was reunited with God halfway through the Rajab [seventh month of the Muslim calendar] of the year 684. May God rest his soul.' From this inscription we learn that Ateş-baz Veli was called Yusuf and that he died in the year 1285. According to Mevlevi legends and popular belief, Ateş-baz Veli was a saint who achieved oneness with God through self-denial. The following tale is told about him: One day Ateş-baz Veli said to Hazreti Mevlana, 'There is no more wood left to light the stove.' Mevlana told him to place his feet under the stove. Ateş-baz Veli did as he was bid. The flames that burst from his toes set the pot boiling immediately. However, because he had entertained doubts about this, his big left toe burned. Mevlana was informed of the event and arrived at the scene, saying sadly, 'Well really, Ateş-baz.' To hide his burnt toe Ateş-baz Veli covered it with the big toe of his right foot. This incident is recalled by Mevlevis during the sema, which begins with the Sufis covering their left toe with their right.

At the first International Food Congress organised by Feyzi Halıcı to commemorate the 700th anniversary of Ateş-baz Veli's death, some of the world's best-known food authorities who came to Konya, visited Ateş-baz Veli's tomb and were fascinated to see his memorial tombstone built in the thirteenth century. One expert, Alan Davidson, wrote in his article 'The Seven Wonders of Konya' after visiting Ateş-baz Veli's tomb, 'Arriving tourists . . . we left like true pilgrims.'

Today it is believed that a sick person who visits Ateş-baz Veli's work place will be healed; also, that taking a pinch of the salt from there to one's own kitchen will bring prosperity and guarantee excellent results.

Table Setting

The food was spread out on low tables close to ground level. At mealtimes it was laid out in the kitchen on round wooden trays set on three-legged trestles, pelts were placed around it and a long cloth tucked underneath the tray stretching all the way round. The spoons were set face down with the handles towards the right. A pinch of salt was placed before each person. The disciples in charge of serving water prepared the jugs. When the preparations had been completed one of the disciples would go to the corridor where the cells were located and invite all to eat by calling out 'Huuu, somata salaaa' ('The table is spread').

The Mevlevis also used another kind of table cover, made of leather, known as 'elifi somat', because it was long like the letter *elif.* It was probably laid out length-wise in the kitchen or the *meydan* when there were a lot of guests for dinner. These covers had slits for slotting in spoons. The disciples sat facing one another at the elifi somat. After the meal, this leather tablecloth was wiped with soapy water, dried, folded and put away.

Celaleddin Çelebi describes meal preparations as follows:

> The food prepared in the Matbah Şerif (Holy Kitchen) was handed out to the Somat Şerif (the dining room) through a small window. The novices' service covered this area too. In short, the Tablesetter's duty consisted of the following:
>
> There were two meals a day in the Somat Şerif, one at eleven o'clock, the other immediately after the evening prayers. The most senior dervish would stand at the door and repeat 'Lokmaya Sala' three times, before completing the invitation to come and eat with 'Huu'. With his hands folded, laid one on top of the other beneath the navel he would wait for all his fellow dervishes to gather inside. He would salute each passing disciple with a gesture of

the head. Inside there were round tables fifty centimetres from the ground seating between ten and twelve people. The disciples would sit on the floor on rush mats. There was a long cloth or oilcloth placed on the knees, 70-80cm wide, stretching all the way round the table. Three slices of bread and a pinch of salt were placed before each person and in the middle of the table there was a spoon turned away from the heart, like the minute hand at ten o'clock.

Table Etiquette

As with the kitchen, food also has sacred characteristics in the Mevlevi tradition. There are special regulations governing its cooking, preparation and eating.

When the food was cooked, the Kazancı Dede (Keeper of the Cauldron and master of service) removed the lid from the cauldron or pot, the novices carrying out kitchen duties lowered the pot to the floor, and the Kazancı Dede chanted the following prayer:

May it be sweet,
May God make it plentiful,
By the breath of Hazreti Mevlana,
By the mystery of Ateş-baz Veli,
Let us chant Hu.

and the disciples chanted 'Hu' together. The disciples who came in response to the invitation to eat entered the kitchen and bowed their heads. The meal started when the sheikh arrived and began and ended with salt. Everyone touched his right index finger first to the tongue, then to the salt, tasted the salt, and then began to eat. All ate from a communal dish. Nobody spoke during the meal. If anyone wanted water he would signal to the novice waiting in the humble position of *muhur*, with the right toe covering the left. The novice would immediately fill the cup with water, kiss it and present it to the disciple who had requested it, who would then kiss it in return before drinking. Whenever anyone was drinking water the others would stop eating and wait so that they would not have taken a single mouthful more than the other disciple. The Sufi who was drinking water would kiss the cup as before and return it to the cup-bearer. The sheikh, or in his absence, the most senior dervish at the table, would say, 'Aşk olsun' ('May it become love') to the Sufi who had drunk and, who would respond with a humble gesture of respect (niyaz). The meal would then be resumed. Apart from the chanted prayer, this was the only word that was spoken at the table. At the end of the meal they would recite this couplet: 'We are the Sufis on this path, we are the ones who eat at the sultan's table, God, make this bowl, this table eternal' and the following prayer:

> [O God] Bestow blessings and peace upon the most gnostic light of all the prophets and divine messengers [Muhammad]. All gratitude is due to God, the Lord of all worlds; [all present invoke] the Fatiha.

After the recital of the Fatiha the pilav would be served and the following prayer chanted:

> Our gratitude to God, thanks be to God, may God grant His blessing, may the abundant dining tables, the bread and blessed food of the enlightened souls be increased. May the spirits of the noble ones among those who have done charitable works and who have passed on be happy and laughing and may those who remain be in sound health. May blessed moments free from worry and times of shared purity be ever greater. By the breath of Hazret-i Mevlana, by the mystery of Ateş-baz Veli, his beneficence İmam-ı Ali, let us chant Hu: Hu.

During the chanting of the prayer, the hands were closed into fists and placed on the edge of the table. After the prayer they would eat the pilav and afterwards the sheikh would bow his head down towards the table, make a humble gesture of entreaty (niyaz), and rise, followed by the others. Once they rose from the table, a bowl and water pitcher was brought for washing the hands. Then, bowing their heads towards the kitchen, they went out. Celaleddin Çelebi describes table etiquette in the following way:

> The novices in charge of serving the table placed the food in the centre. The words 'Bismillahirrahmanirrahim', spoken by the most senior dervish present, were the signal for the meal to begin. The meal began and ended with salt licked off the end of the right index finger. Novices would stand against a wall close to the table with hands folded, laid one on top of the other below the navel, waiting to serve. Disciples communicated their needs to them with a look. The meal was conducted in

> silence. Anyone requiring water would inform the novice with a look. The novice would carefully fill the cup and present it. The thirsty Sufi would take the cup, bring it to his lips, kiss it, say, 'Bismillahirrahmanirrahim' and drink. Meanwhile, the others seated at the table would withdraw their hands from the table and wait. The Sufi who had drunk water would kiss the side of the cup once again and return it; the novice who had served him would kiss the cup in the same way and stand aside. It was the novices' duty to change and replenish the communal serving dish in the centre.

A disciple who had eaten his fill was not free to leave the table, but would turn his spoon over to its original position and wait. When the sounds of spoons had died down and there was an atmosphere of calm, the second most senior dervish in the Somat would say, 'Bismillah, Eyvallah' (In the name of God we give thanks) and everyone, including those who wished to continue eating, would return their spoons to their original position, balance their fingers on the edges of the table, bow their heads and wait. The disciples would put down everything they were holding, fold their arms diagonally, make a humble gesture of entreaty (niyaz) and wait, with their heads bowed down towards their hearts. At that point total silence reigned in the Somat. It would be broken with the prayers of the most senior dervish. The prayer began with a couplet from Hazret-i Mevlana's *Divan-ı Kebir:* '. . .We are the Sufis who have set out on the path, those who live on God's provisions. Oh Lord, make this table eternal . . .' After this prayer they would all recite the Fatiha together, and then recite a prayer of thanks. For example, 'Manı

Merdan, Himmeti Yezdan, berekatı Halil-ül Rahman. May the morsels we have eaten become light and faith. May our hearts overflow with Divine Love with every breath we take. May our praise and gratitude be eternal, our cheer everlasting. By the breath of Hazreti Mevlana, by the mystery of Şems-i Veled, the Light of Muhammad, the Mystery of Ateş-baz Veli, let us chant Hu, Huuuu …' After this prayer anyone who wished to do so could rise, saluting the disciples at his table with his hand on his heart and a gesture of the head. He would walk out of the door backwards, so he was facing the disciples at the other tables, and salute them in the same way. Once the Somat was emptied the novices would clear away the platters and hand them over to the novices in the Matbah (kitchen), wipe the tablecloths, sweep the floor and leave the Somat.

Food

As far as food is concerned, it can be said that the cuisine was shaped by the products of the era. We know from the *Histories of the Seljuks* that palace cuisine was spectacular at the time when Mevlana arrived in the capital, Konya, with his family. The H.T.H. edition of the *History of the Seljuks* speaks of food – pilavs, zerdes (sweet, saffron puddings), kalyes (meat and/or vegetables cooked with onions and butter), boranis (vegetable dishes with yogurt and rice), helvas, yahnis (lamb stews with tomatoes and onions), biryans (probably the lamb dish cooked in a tandır oven known as çebiç in Konya), grilled chicken, pigeon, partridge and quail – prepared and served on lavishly decorated earthenware and gold platters, when Aladdin Keykubad I arrived in Konya as its ruler. It also mentions that koumiss (fermented mare's or other milk) and several varieties of sherbet were served at this meal. Mevlana also writes about the same dishes in his works. It is clear that in that era game birds were a delicacy served only at exclusive tables.

It is likely that in Mevlana's time meals prepared with more basic ingredients, as in folk cuisine, eventually found their way into the dergah kitchens. In his works Mevlana mentions spices such as cumin, black pepper, cinnamon and sumach. The gradual introduction of other spices, the addition of pekmez (grape syrup) to meat dishes and the use of sweet and sour flavours such as pekmez and vinegar together in certain dishes enhanced their flavour. The courgettes still prepared in Konya, using verjuice (unripe grape juice) or vinegar and pekmez together, is one example of the sweet–sour melange. Dishes such as sweet butternut squash and gerdan tatlısı (a dessert typically prepared at the Feast of the Sacrifice, made from the chuck meat of lamb) are examples of the combination of sweet and savoury. Ali Eşref Dede's pumpkin kalye also shows that dergah kitchens probably used the sweet–sour combination between the thirteenth and nineteenth centuries.

Ali Eşref Dede's treatise is yet another demonstration of the fact that Sufi cuisine was more refined than folk cuisine.

I have been told that they added gold dust to sherbet in the palace. The kadayıf mücver with gold vark, however, which I have included in this book, is an exquisite recipe that I have not found in any cookbook. This again shows that dergah cuisine was as select as palace cuisine.

Fish is said to be prohibited in Mevlevi cuisine but in the *Divan-ı Kebir* Mevlana, expounding on the extensive hospitality lavished on one particular guest, describes the exquisite fish he was offered as follows: 'Each day was better than the last; he served enticing fish, as enticing as our beauteous maidens' (dl:379-b:3479-80). Mevlana also mentions fried fish in his other works. It is only Gölpınarlı, in his book about Mevlevi teachings and practices, written after Mevlana's death, who writes, on the basis of the testimony of the sheikh of Bahariye Mevlevihane, Hüseyin Fakhreddin Dede, that no fish ever enters a Mevlevi kitchen. Ali Eşref Dede, on the other hand, gives many fish recipes, from salad to fried fish, and stew to grilled fillets. It is possible that fish, in wide use during Mevlana's era, was removed from Sufi dergahs for some reason and reintroduced later.

In his work entitled *Mevlevi Teachings After Mevlana* Gölpınarlı writes that Mevlevis called food 'lokma' (a syrup-filled fried dumpling) and mentions the existence of a certain pilav that they refer to as 'exceptionally lokma'. The author explains that this is the Balkh-Özbek pilav originating from Mevlana's era, made from onions, carrots, chestnuts and heavily marbled meat.

Cooking Methods Used in Sufi Cuisine

There are four main cooking methods used in Mevlevi cuisine, with various subdivisions. One, cooking in water. This includes boiling and steaming, as with söğüş meat (meat cooked by boiling and then served cold). Steaming is rarely used in classic Turkish cuisine although Ali Eşref Dede's book contains a recipe for steamed pilav. In Turkish folk cuisine, in Çorum, İskilip pilav is also prepared using this method. Two, frying – shallow and deep. Vegetables, for example, are shallow fried, whereas lokma and similar dishes are deep fried. Three, cooking in dry heat. This includes cooking in the oven, the saç, under the grill, közleme (grilling food in hot ashes or over embers) and in the tandır. Four, cooking with a combination of fat and water. This covers all stews and casseroles, such as those classified under yahni (stew made with onions and tomatoes), bastı (vegetable stew), musakka and dolma.

Preparation of the Book

The first stage of preparation for this book was to go through Mevlana's complete works and lift out all the food, drink and dishes he mentions. In part one of the recipe section I have standardised the recipes that appear in his works (in the past quantities and cooking times were not as specific as they are in modern recipes).

I have taken many of the recipes for part two, dishes mentioned in his works, recipes that live on in the cuisine of Konya and which are from my earlier books about Konya.

Otherwise they have been collected from the old ladies who are keeping the tradition alive, and standardised. To recreate the authentic flavour of that era I have retested and standardised the recipes that still exist in Konya cuisine, using the ingredients available in Mevlana's time.

In Mevlana's time olive oil and sesame oil were used as fuel for oil lamps. For this reason, with the exception of the recipes taken from Ali Eşref Dede, the recipes use the fats of that era, such as butter, sheep's-tail fat and clarified butter.

I have substituted the tomato puree that is used in recipes today for plums or koruk (unripe grapes), which gave food its sour flavour before tomato puree came into use. I have also included today's methods for preparing the dishes. I have used only the spices that Mevlana refers to in his works.

With the exception of cabbage soup, liver soup, pickled turnip, sirkencübin (honey mixed with vinegar), gülbeşeker şemsiyesi, sweet spinach and barley bread, all the dishes mentioned by Mevlana have survived in Konya cuisine to the present day.

I have included certain dishes still prepared in Konya, such as su börek (cheese-filled pastry cooked first in water, then baked in the oven), saç börek and baked carp, which are not mentioned in the works but are nevertheless likely to have existed in that era. I have indicated whereever this has been the case.

The third part contains dishes found in Eflaki, but not in Mevlana's works. Ali Eşref Dede's dishes, which comprise part four, are completely faithful renditions of the recipes in his work. The development of the select Mevlevi cuisine that continued from the thirteenth to the nineteenth century, ranging from yahni and helva to stuffed melon and kadayıf with gold vark, is thus displayed before you.

The standardised dishes were appraised by a panel of experts from Konya and then registered.

I have included couplets from Mevlana's works relevant to particular dishes, at the beginning of the recipe; couplets related to food and drink appear at the end of this book.

Please take the following points into consideration when preparing the dishes:

— In Mevlevi cuisine, as in Turkish cuisine, copper pots that distributed heat evenly were used.The use of copper being rare today, the recipes were tested in steel pans.
— If no other implement is indicated, use a wooden spoon.
— For dishes such as helva and soup, which call for flour and fat to be cooked slowly, use a round-bottomed saucepan.
— The most important characteristic of both Turkish and Mevlevi cuisines is that the food is cooked on a low heat without spoiling its shape.
— While pilav and helva are steeping, and when preparing dishes cooked with small quantities of water, shake the saucepan from time to time to prevent the food burning.
— Both Turkish and Sufi cuisines generally use tender meat such as mutton and lamb. You may substitute beef, in which case you can add a tablespoon of wine vinegar during cooking to achieve the same tenderness.
— If pastry dough is too soft or too hard, it can be corrected by adding a little flour or water, milk or the liquid used in the dough.
— Follow the given measurements when preparing syrup for desserts. If you increase the amount of sugar, it will crystallise; if you decrease it, the dessert will be doughy.

— Similarly, when preparing syrups for desserts stick to the times given. Over-boiled syrup forms crystals.
— We know that in Mevlana's time sweets were prepared with honey or pekmez (grape syrup). You may use pekmez as it is. The best honey is that sold with the honeycomb, but this must be strained. To strain honey, place a sieve over a bowl. Pour the honey with the honeycomb into the sieve and leave it overnight. The honey that has been strained into the bowl underneath can then be used as required.
— Bring syrup prepared with honey, or any desserts to which you have added honey, to the boil only once and then remove from heat. If you over-boil it, the honey will turn bitter and will spoil the taste of the syrup or dessert.
— In Mevlana's time, and until much later, butter was the fat most often used for cooking. Olive and sesame oil were used for lamps. Writing in the nineteenth century, Ali Eşref Dede uses oil in some of his recipes, and if you wish to substitute sunflower oil for part of the butter used in the recipes, you may do so. I suggest sunflower oil because it is neutral in smell and taste. However, do not use oil when making baklava, börek and other pastries, pasta or pilav because the flavour and texture provided by a solid fat is needed. If you want to make a substitute in these recipes, it would be better to use margarine.

  The fat of the fat-tailed sheep is also used, either melted, strained and used for frying, or cut in small cubes for kebabs. You could use fat from other parts for kebabs, and butter or oil as a substitute for frying (see above).
— You may vary the proportions of oil, tomato puree, salt and spices according to your taste.
— Use steel pans lined with tin, or stainless steel or enamel

pans for preparing dishes with milk or yogurt, to avoid discolouration of the utensils.

— If dishes containing yogurt require further cooking after the yogurt has been added, cook without a cover, stirring in one direction only, otherwise it may curdle.

— Dishes containing yogurt are not generally re-heated, but if you have leftovers that need heating do so on a low heat without covering the pan, stirring continuously.

RECIPES FROM MEVLANA'S WORKS

Fried Fish

'I am like a fish in the market, in the bazaar, in the pan, flipping from one side to the other, turning over and over, I burn and blaze.'
2:106-C:869

'By the grace of Hızır even the fried fish came back to life and leapt into the sea, where it made its choice.' M6:408-C:2646

In Mevlana's era it is likely that improved communications would have made it possible to eat fish caught in Lakes Beyşehir and Seydişehir. It is baked in the oven as well as fried.

Serves 4

— 1kg or 2lb 4oz Beyşehir carp
— Salt to taste
— 2 tbsps plain flour
— Vinegar for marinating
— 500g or 2 cups clarified butter (for frying)

Clean and descale the fish and cut into slices approximately 2cm thick, or divide into 4 fillets. Marinate in vinegar for 1 hour. Remove from the vinegar, sprinkle with salt and place in a sieve.

Heat the butter, coat the fish with flour and add to the hot fat. When it is brown on one side flip it over and fry the other side. Drain in a sieve, place in a dish and serve.

To accompany: Onion piyaz with sumach (see glossary)

Sweet Buttery Soup

Bulamaç Aşı

'But when your soul is intoxicated it has no desire even for that food; will anyone drunk on the contemplation of your face ever look at bulamaç aş?' D1:318-C:2941

'Love's maturity lies in the union of the lover and the beloved; come hither, blend into one another and fuse together, like the bulamaç aş that is born when fat and flour blend into one another until they become inseparable.' D3:228-C:2131

In Konya bulamaç is called 'ahead of the bride'. On the wedding day the mother of the girl getting married prepares bulamaç while her daughter is preparing to leave her father's house for her new home. She sends it to the boy's house with an old woman before her daughter arrives, so that she may be surrounded by sweetness in her new home.

Bulamaç is eaten with chunks of bread dipped into it. It is delicious with any sweetener. I particularly recommend bulamaç made with freshly strained honey.

Serves 4

— 125g or generous ½ cup clarified butter (see glossary)
— 50g or ½ cup strong plain flour
— 125g or ¼ cup pekmez (see glossary), strained honey or sugar (can be increased or decreased, according to taste)
— 400ml or 1 ¾ cups water
— 5 tbsps butter, to garnish
— Yufka or tandır bread (see glossary)

Melt the clarified butter in a pan. Add the flour and mix well. Cook over a very low heat for approximately 60 minutes (the longer it cooks the better it will taste) until golden brown. Bring the water to a boil and pour in the pekmez or honey, stirring continuously. Add to the flour mixture. (If using sugar, mix it with cold water, bring to the boil, remove from the heat immediately and pour into the flour mixture.) Keep stirring until it is the consistency of thickset yogurt. Pour into a dish. Heat the butter and drizzle over the top. Serve hot with yufka or tandır bread.

Rose Jam

Gülbeşeker

'O rose who escaped from the rose garden to fuse with sugar,
how could you abandon the rose garden?' DI:13-C:73

'Now you have become gülbeşeker you are food of the heart,
light of the eyes, stop yearning after the rose now,
it is leagues away from all of this.' DI:13-C:16

'They eat even the bitter-tasting victuals of command, digesting them as though they were gülbeşeker.' M3:259-C:2347

This recipe is used for preparing jam in Konya. Fresh rose petals are used. The petals are preserved by mixing with sugar and placing in jars, to be used as required for jam or sherbet. The first ever published book of Turkish cuisine, known as *Melceü't Tabbahin*, describes gülbeşeker as rose jam. The gülbeşeker mentioned by Mevlana is likely to have been either rose jam or candied rose petals. In the same book this recipe is referred to as gülbeşeker şemsiyesi (umbrella). I have therefore included the recipes for rose jam, preserved rose petals and gülbeşeker şemsiyesi, which is not prepared in Konya and Anatolia.

Although it is preferable to use fresh petals for this recipe, preserved petals that have been mixed with sugar and packed into a jar may also be used.

— 125g or 1 cup fresh, fragrant, pink, ever-blooming rose petals
— Juice of 2 lemons
— 1kg or 4 ½ cups granulated sugar
— 600ml or 2 ½ cups water

Remove the white base of the rose petals with a pair of scissors. Place the petals in a large glass or porcelain bowl. Add the lemon juice and rub it in by hand for 10 minutes, then set aside for 20 minutes.

Place the water and sugar in a heavy pan over the fire and bring it to the boil. Turn the heat down and boil for another two minutes. Add the rose petals and cook for another two minutes.

Remove from the heat and pour into a glass or porcelain bowl. Cover with gauze.

Place the bowl in sunlight during the day, to bring the jam to the correct consistency. If you are in a climate with insufficient sunlight, simmer the rose petals on a low heat until they have softened. The jam is ready when it becomes 'stringy' when stretched between finger and thumb. Transfer the jam into jars and store in a cool place.

Candied Rose Petals

Gülbeşeker Şemsiyesi (Umbrella)

'Your mother is a radish, your father a turnip,
beside them you are gülbeşeker.' Anon

This proverb, used very frequently in Konya to poke fun at those who give themselves airs and graces and ignore their humble origins, shows that gülbeşeker originates from that era, although it has not survived to the present day.

— 500g or 2 ¼ cups granulated sugar
— 250g or 2 cups pink, fragrant, ever-blooming rose petals

Remove the white base of the rose petals with a pair of scissors. Place the petals in a big bowl, rub the sugar into them thoroughly by hand and transfer to covered glass jars. Put the jars on a copper tray. On hot days remove the covers and take the jars out into the sun. Continue this process for approximately one month, until the rose petals have solidified and resemble transparent candy.

Preserving Rose Petals
— 1kg or 4 ½ cups granulated sugar
— 250g or 2 cups pink, fragrant, ever-blooming rose petals

Remove the white edges of the rose petals with a pair of scissors. In a big bowl, rub the sugar into them thoroughly by hand and transfer them to glass jars. Store in a cool place and use as required for sherbet or jam.

Aubergine Salad

'Who are the aubergine's friends? Vinegar and garlic.' D3:459-B:4400

'It is no surprise if an unbeliever is sour,
aubergines have a rapport with sourness.' D4:209-B:1955

Aubergines are very popular in Konya. Sometimes they are served sliced, with butter. Nowadays we add olive oil to this salad.

Serves 4

— ½ kg or 1lb 2oz aubergine 2 cloves garlic
— Salt to taste
— 100ml or ½ cup wine vinegar

Prick the aubergines several times with a knife. Roast them on a brazier for 30 minutes until tender. When cool enough to handle, peel and chop them finely and place in a dish.

Crush the garlic with the salt and beat it with the vinegar. Pour over the salad and serve.

Honey and Vinegar

Sirkencübin

'If there is less honey than vinegar the sirkencübin will not be right.'

M6:7-C:19

(Sirkencübin is no longer prepared today.)

Serves 4

— 4 tsps honey
— 4 tsps wine vinegar 800ml or 3 ⅓ cups water

Mix the vinegar, honey and water. Pour into glasses and serve.

Clarified Butter

'Inform his kindness and beneficence, that they may serve this man clarified butter at dinner.' D5:178-C:2020

This dish is eaten hot with chunks of bread dipped into it. Alternatively, it can be poured over, and rubbed into, small pieces of tandır bread.

Serves 4
— 250g or 2 ½ sticks butter

To accompany
— Tandır or yufka bread, or bazlama (see pp. 139, 141 and 137)

Place the butter in a pan, heat for 5–10 minutes until it is a golden brown colour. Pour into a warmed dish leaving behind the white residue. Serve with tandır or yufka bread, or bazlama.

DISHES MENTIONED IN MEVLANA'S WORKS STILL PREPARED IN KONYA TODAY

Soups

'Bring food from the heavens, like a Messiah;
that the people may renounce this bread and soup.'
D2:395-C:3300

'Strangle fame with hunger; do not get excited over soup.'
D5:364-C:4694

'You fast too and await that table laden with rapture and joy;
that table of kindness is certainly better than cabbage soup.'
D3:258

'You are intolerant; if you approach those eating liver
and are transformed into liver they will seize you
and toss you into their soup.' D3:116-C:955

Mevlana talked about cabbage and liver soup, as well as the soups listed below. While cabbage soup still survives in the Karadeniz region, and liver soup in Istanbul cuisine, neither exists any longer in Konya cuisine. As liver soup appears in Ali Eşref Dede's treatise, I have included it in that section, but I have not included cabbage soup. Mevlana certainly spoke of cornbread from Karadeniz, but it is probable that cornbread was either prepared in Konya as well at that time or that a disciple from Karadeniz prepared it in the dergah kitchen.

Meat Stock

— 2.4 litres or 10 cups water
— ½ kg or 1lb 2oz scrag end of neck of lamb, lamb breast, leg of lamb or 2kg or 4 ½ lb bones
— 1 onion peeled
— 1 carrot
— 1 tbsp rice
— 3 whole black peppercorns
— 1 tsp salt

Place the meat or bones in a large saucepan with the cold water and put on to heat. When it comes to a boil skim off the foam that forms on the surface. Add the washed vegetables, rice and black pepper. Return the saucepan to the fire and again bring to the boil. Lower the heat and simmer for approximately one hour. Add the salt and remove from the heat. Strain. If too much liquid has evaporated, add enough hot water to make 2 litres of meat stock.

Tripe Soup

'For example, when a man's guest fancies tripe soup …' FM:116

'Because it did not reach for vinegary soup the world was given strength by the Messiah.'
Eflaki, *The Book of the Wise 2.* S.130

Tripe soup is still prepared in Konya today. At Kurban Bayram (The Feast of the Sacrifice) in particular, it is made in every home where there has been a sacrifice. Today cayenne pepper is sprinkled on top. It is served with lemon.

Serves 4
— 250g or 1 heaped cup cleaned, washed tripe
— 1 litre or 4 ½ cups water
— Salt to taste
— 2 tbsps clarified butter or butter
— 2 tbsps plain flour

For the sauce
— 100ml or ½ cup wine vinegar
— 6 cloves garlic
— Salt
— 1 tbsp clarified butter, to garnish
— ½ teaspoon cumin, mint or cinnamon

Place the tripe in a saucepan with the water and put on to heat. When it comes to a boil skim the foam that has formed on the surface, cover and boil for approximately 2 hours (1 hour in a pressure cooker) until it is tender. Add the salt and remove from the heat after 5 minutes. Strain over a bowl. If necessary, add water to make up 1 litre.

Finely chop the tripe.

Melt the butter in a pan. Add the flour, stirring continuously. Continue to cook until the flour is lightly coloured. Do not allow it to brown. Add the cooled tripe stock, stirring all the time. When it comes to a boil add the tripe, cover, lower the heat and simmer for another 5 minutes.

Place the vinegar in a bowl. Crush the garlic with the salt and mix with the vinegar. Add to the boiling soup. Add salt if necessary. Cook for another 5 minutes and pour into a soup tureen.

Heat the butter in a pan and drizzle over the soup. Sprinkle the cumin, mint or cinnamon over the top and serve with tandır bread.

Lentil Soup

'Thanks be to God I say; then I ask what did you eat, he says I drank sherbet, or I ate lentil soup.' MI:557-C:3378

This delicious soup is found not only in Konya but in many other parts of Anatolia too, with slight variations. Today we add cayenne pepper as well as the mint.

Serves 4

— 150g or 1 ½ cups brown or green lentils
— 600ml or 2 ½ cups water (for boiling)

- 1 litre or 4 cups meat stock
- 75g or ½ cup erişte (homemade pasta, see p. 205)
- 2 tbsps clarified butter
- 1 onion, finely chopped
- 1 tbsp plain flour
- 1 tsp mint
- Salt to taste

Wash the lentils and put on to heat in a saucepan with the 600ml of water. When it comes to a boil turn down the heat and simmer for 40 minutes. Strain the water.

Place the hot meat stock and lentils in a casserole. When it boils add the pasta. Melt the butter in a small frying pan and brown the onions. Add the flour and cook until it also turns golden brown, add to the soup. Add the mint, salt to taste and cover. Simmer on a very low heat for approximately one hour, until it has thickened. Serve in the casserole.

Tandır Soup

'If you are inept at casting pot to fire and cooking soup, be assured that fire and sparks will wreck both pot and soup.' M5:239-C:1379

In Konya, in households with tandırs, tandır soup is invariably prepared in the evening of the day they bake tandır bread. All the ingredients are placed in the çömlek (earthenware pot) raw, lowered into the tandır and eaten for lunch the following day. Today, if you prepare your soup on the stove you will get better results if you follow the recipe below. Nowadays we also add cayenne pepper to the soup.

Serves 5 or more

— 38g or ⅛ cup chick peas
— 38g or ⅛ cup white kidney beans
— 2 onions, finely chopped
— 2 tbsps clarified butter
— 75g or ⅓ cup bulgur wheat
— 75g or ⅓ cup green lentils
— 2 tbsps kavurma, prepared with meat chopped using the 'bıçak arası' technique
— 1.6 litres or 6 ½ cups meat stock
— 1 tsp cumin
— 1 tsp black pepper
— Salt to taste

Soak the chick peas and white kidney beans in water for eight hours. Fry the onions in the clarified butter until golden brown. Add the bulgur wheat and stir. Add the lentils, chick peas, white kidney beans, spices, meat and meat stock. Bring to a boil, cover and turn the heat down to low. Cook for approximately two hours until the beans and chick peas are tender. Add salt to taste, cook for another 10 minutes and remove from the heat. Leave to stand for 10-20 minutes and serve in the casserole.

Tarhana Soup

'As you refuse to leave this world for the tavern of life, drink tasteless, insipid tarhana soup in place of wine.' D4:429-C:4152

This couplet shows that tarhana soup had a lowly status in that era. Konya cuisine has some delicious soups. Perhaps for this reason Konya, being the capital reflecting Seljuk culture, makes little use of tarhana soup today. It is found more frequently outside the capital.

Serves 4–6

— 125g or 5oz tarhana
— 400 ml or 1 ¾ cups water (for soaking)
— 1 litre or 4 cups meat stock
— 2 cloves garlic
— Salt to taste
— 1 tsp dry mint
— 2 tbsps clarified butter

Soak the tarhana overnight. In the morning crumble it by hand, without crushing it. Put it in a saucepan together with the meat stock. Cook on a medium heat, stirring continuously, for 10–15 minutes, until it has thickened. Grind the garlic with the salt and add to the tarhana. Bring to the boil and transfer it to a soup tureen. Heat the clarified butter and add the mint. When the mint expands remove from the heat immediately, to prevent it from discolouring. Sprinkle on to the soup and serve.

Tutmaç Soup

'Like a steam-misted cauldron, you pursue tutmaç; where is the greatness born of honouring the Almighty's secret? Where the kingly support and effort?' D2:246-C:2109

'Across the land Turkish mothers, sisters pray
To eat food obtained in a lawful way
Central Asia to Anatolia we've stretched,
And the divine taste of tutmaç is not one we'll forget.'
Feyzi Halıcı

This is a delicious soup, often mentioned in Mevlana's works, which is still prepared in Konya. Its origin is explained as follows in the *Divanü Lügat-it Turk*, a dictionary compiled by Kaşgarlı Mahmut designed to teach Turkish to the Arabs: 'Tutmaç: a well known Turkish dish. It was prepared in the era of Zülkarneyn. When he emerged from the dark [the war] his food supplies were low. His people complained to him of their hunger: 'Bizi tutma aç' ['Don't keep us hungry'] they said, and he ordered this dish to be prepared for them, hence the name.' Kaşgarlı also talks about the fact that the resin of the *Ferula szowitsiana DC umbelliferae* tree is added to the yogurt for tutmaç to give it a red colour. In

Konya tutmaç is the colour of yogurt. Sprinkling mint on the top will turn it green.

It is possible to make tutmaç without frying the dough in oil, using winter erişte. In this case you can boil the dough directly with the cooked meat. Using strained yogurt from Konya will give you the authentic flavour.

Serves 5 or more

For the dough

— 100g or 1 level cup strong plain flour (adjust according to the size of the egg)
— 1 egg
— ½ an eggshell of water
— ½ tsp salt

To fry the dough and the pastry croutons

— 200g or 1 cup clarified butter

For the soup

— 250g or 9oz lamb, cut into small chunks
— 1 litre or 1 ¾ pints of water
— 1 portion of tutmaç dough, as above
— 250ml or 1 cup (preferably) Konya thick set strained yogurt
— 1 egg
— 1 tbsp plain flour
— 200ml or 1 cup water
— 2 cloves garlic
— ½ tsp salt

To boil the pasta

— 800 ml or 3 ⅓ cups water
— 1 tsp salt
— 1 tbsp clarified butter

For the pastry croûtons

— 50g or ½ cup plain flour
— 1 egg
— ¼ tsp salt

To garnish

— 1 tbsp butter
— ½ tsp mint

Knead the flour, egg, water and salt until you have a soft, pliable dough. Cover with a damp cloth and leave to stand for 20 minutes. Roll out two sheets of dough the thickness of a knife blade (3mm). Cut rectangular strips measuring 2mm x 3cm (you will get approx 200g dough). Leave to air on a cloth for half an hour. Fry half the dough in 100ml of clarified butter and strain.

To make the soup

Boil 1 litre of water in a saucepan. Add the meat. Do not cover. When it begins to boil skim off the foam that forms on the surface, cover and cook on a medium heat for about an hour, until the meat is tender. Add the salt. Remove from the heat after 5 minutes. If the water has evaporated top up to make a total of 1 litre.

To cook the pasta

Boil the water, salt and clarified butter in a separate saucepan. Add the fried tutmaç dough. Cook on a medium heat until the dough is soft, about 15 minutes. Strain.

To make the pastry croûtons, knead the flour, egg and salt in a bowl. Roll out into a long sausage. Cut the dough into lentil-sized pieces. Fry in 100g of clarified butter and strain.

In a bowl, beat the yogurt, egg, flour and water. Peel the garlic and grind it with a little salt, adding it to the yogurt mixture. Take some of the water from the soup and add to the yogurt mixture until it is the same consistency as crêpe batter. Stirring continuously, pour into the cooking meat. Mix the boiled, strained tutmaç into the soup slowly. Stirring continuously always in the same direction, bring to the boil several times. Add more salt if necessary and transfer to a soup tureen.

Heat the butter in a frying pan, add the mint and remove from the heat after less than a minute (the mint should remain green and not turn black) and sprinkle over the soup. Sprinkle a few pastry croûtons over the top. Place any extra croûtons in a dish and serve with the soup.

Mezes

'Crystalline wine arrived, followed by almonds for meze,
honey and sugar.' D5:273-C:3196

'The languidness of love serves wine in the grave, summons beauties,
lights candles, presents kebab, prepares meze,
lights incense as a gift for you.' D3:-C:1860

'Eventually your beloved becomes your bread and your water,
your lighting candle and your beauty,
your meze and your wine.' M4:4611-C:2

Mevlana mentioned only almonds, honey and sugar as meze, nothing else. In this section I have therefore included only related couplets.

Eggs

'A young philosopher who believed in nature thought the sky looked like an egg and the earth like its yolk.' M:445-C:2472

'Time is an egg, and so is the earth.' D4:74-C:639

'You may be certain that faith with blasphemy is like the white and yolk of this egg; there is a barzakh[1] *separating them, they do not mix.'* D4:74-C:640

Pancakes

Lalanga

'In the village there will be bread, lalanga,
lavish dishes, for great and small alike.' M3:404-C:3346

Lalanga may be sweet or savoury. You can make savoury lalanga by adding 50g lalanga cheese and a pinch of salt to the ingredients below. I have adapted the recipe from Ali Eşref Dede, giving a raising agent which could have been used in the thirteenth century. You may use any raising agent you wish. Nowadays this type of fried dish can be prepared with olive oil.

Serves 4

— *For the raising agent*
— 1 tbsp yogurt
— 1 tsp thick cream
— ¼ tsp honey

— 50ml or ¼ cup water
— 2 tbsps plain flour

For the syrup
— 250g or 1 ½ cups honey strained without heating
— 200ml or 1 cup water

For the lalanga
— 2 eggs
— 100ml or ½ cup water

Raising agent (see above)
— 100g or 1 level cup strong plain flour

To fry
— 250g or 1 cup clarified butter

Beat the ingredients for the raising agent in a bowl the night before, cover and leave in a warm place.

Boil the water, add the honey, stirring continuously, till it comes to a boil.

Remove from the heat immediately. Cool.

Beat the ingredients for the lalanga in a porcelain bowl, cover and leave in a warm place for one hour. Heat the clarified butter in a small frying pan (15cm diameter) and ladle small quantities of the batter into the hot fat. When one side has browned turn the lalanga over and brown the other side. Put into the syrup and leave until the next lalanga has cooked. Arrange on a plate and serve.

Eggs with Kavurma

This is a delicious dish and one that best recalls that era. It is also a good dish to make when you are in a hurry. Prepare it with the kavurma you already have at home, with meat chopped according to the bıçak arası (see glossary) technique.

Because kavurma is salty there is no extra salt in this dish, but if you wish you can add a little to the eggs. Nowadays this recipe is also prepared with minced meat kavurma.

Serves 4

— ½ kg or 1lb 2oz of lamb kavurma (see p. 161)
— 1 onion, finely chopped
— 4 eggs
— Black pepper to sprinkle on top

To accompany

— Ayran (see p. 145)
— Cress, mint, spring onions, radishes and similar crisp vegetables

Fry the kavurma and onions in a frying pan until the onions are golden brown. Transfer to a heatproof dish or baking tin. Make four wells, break the eggs into them, cover and cook on a low heat until the whites have solidified. Sprinkle with black pepper and serve in the same dish, accompanied by ayran and a selection of crisp salad vegetables.

Meat

'You are placing roast calf before him.' M3:55-C:400

Mevlana's works mention that the meat from animals such as camels, sheep, goats, calves and cows was eaten As in Konya and elsewhere in Turkey, meat is the most important component of a meal in Mevlevi cuisine. A meal without meat is not considered to be a meal.

Meat with Plums

Calla

'Enough, be silent, words cannot take the place of opinions, as pomegranates and apples cannot take the place of plums.' D5:2-C:334

'You tried to pass an orange as a plum,
but how can an orange ever be a plum?' D5:207-C:2378

Although Mevlana does not speak of calla as such, it is likely that this dish made with plums came from that era and was prepared in dergah kitchens in the same way. I have included it for that reason. The Seljuks used plums or unripe grapes to give food a sour flavour. Calla is one such sour dish still prepared in Konya today. The recipe calls for sour unripe plums. Nowadays we also prepare calla with tomato puree or even, when plums are unavailable, with large quantities of tomatoes.

Serves 4

— ½ kg or 1lb 2oz heavily marbled rib bones
— 600ml or 2 ½ cups water
— 10–15 unripe plums
— 1 tbsp clarified butter
— 2 onions, finely chopped
— Salt to taste

Wash the meat, boil the water, pour it over the meat and cook for approximately one hour, until it is tender and all the water has been absorbed. Score the plums in one or two places and place on top of the meat.

Fry the onions in a pan with the clarified butter. Pour over the meat and plums in the saucepan, add salt and cover. Cook for another 15–20 minutes, until the plums are soft.

Place the meat in a dish with the plums arranged around it and serve.

Meat Roasted in a Clay Pot

Çömlek Kebab

'You abandon that pot at the door where there are rich victuals to be had, and run off in pursuit of a leftover tirit.' M3:46-C:296

Today we add chopped green peppers and tomatoes to this kebab, and cook it either on the stove or in the oven.

Serves 4
— ½ kg or 1lb 2oz lean lamb
— ½ kg or 1lb 2oz aubergines, preferably from Konya

- 2 onions, cut into rings
- 4–5 unripe plums
- 200ml or 1 cup meat stock or water
- Salt to taste

Wash the meat and place it in an earthenware pot. Cut off the green ends of the aubergines and cut them into circular slices without peeling them. Arrange the slices on top of the meat. Add the onions, whole plums and meat stock. Season and cook in the oven, preheated to 200°C for 50–60 minutes. Serve in the earthenware pot.

Neck of Lamb

'That slap you received will be followed by abundance, kindness; wait and see O confident soul; it will come to you with round steak and neck of lamb.' M6:238-C:9

Nowadays neck of lamb is prepared as both a sweet and savoury dish in Konya. Both are delicious. My recipe is for the savoury version but, to give you an idea, I am also including the instructions for a dessert given to me by Hafize Ayvacı from Konya. 'We wash the neck of lamb and boil it well. We add a handful of rice. We add sugar and continue to cook until the rice is soft. If you like you can add a little cinnamon. You can also use pekmez. Adding a glass of boiled neck of lamb to the recipe for zerde (in the dessert section) and cooking it with however much pekmez suits your palate will give you a chance to savour one of the exquisite flavours of Mevlana's era.'

You may like to follow Mevlana's recommendation and add two lamb leg steaks to this savoury recipe.

Serves 4
— 1 neck of lamb
— 800ml or 3 ⅓ cups water
— Salt to taste
— Cinnamon

Wash the meat and place in a saucepan with the water. Skim off the foam that forms on the surface as it is boiling. Cover and boil for 80–90 minutes, until it becomes tender. Add salt to taste, boil for 5 more minutes and remove from heat. Place the lamb in a dish and spoon some of the broth over it. Alternatively, shred the boiled meat, return to its liquid, bring to the boil again and serve in a dish with the broth, sprinkled with cinnamon. Serve with tandır bread.

Diced Kebab

Şiş Kebab

'When the barrels of the wine of love gush, foaming in excitement, when the time has come to eat kebab, the rebap will play.'
D5:268-C:3132

'At that moment the historiographers spread the word; and decorated the skewer with kebab.' M4:265-C:1322

'When he opens the door he renders the spoken word unspoken and neither skewer nor kebab burns.' MI:339-C:1680

It is likely that siş kebab was invented by a tribe of nomadic Turks. They probably threaded the meat of the animals they hunted on to fine twigs and cooked them. The expression still used in Anatolia, also mentioned by Mevlana, 'so neither skewer nor kebab burns' (meaning both parties should be treated fairly, because if one burns, the other may burn too) supports the theory that şiş kebab originated in this way; the twigs used as skewers also caught fire.

Serves 4
— ½ kg or 1lb 2oz leg of lamb cut into cubes
— ½ kg or 1lb 2oz lamb's tail cut into cubes

Thread alternate chunks of meat and tail on to skewers. Place the meat 10cm above the charcoal on a barbecue and cook. Brush the skewers with meat stock from time to time to prevent the meat from drying.

Arrange yufka bread on plates, place the skewers on top and serve accompanied with ayran, spring onion, mint and cress.

Pan Fried Kebab

Tava Kebab

'While Noah attemptd to fry kebab, Lot's wife kept throwing stones in the pan.' M6:666-C:4483

Today in Konya we use every kind of meat and offal to make pan fried kebab.

Serves 4

— ½ kg or 1lb 2oz leg of lamb
— 250g or 1 cup clarified butter or sheep's-tail fat (see p. 40)

Remove the tendons from the meat and cut it into egg-sized pieces. Beat each piece to a thickness of half a centimetre.

Heat the fat in a pan, when hot, add the meat. Fry for 3–4 minutes until one side is browned, then turn over and brown the other side. Arrange on a dish and serve accompanied with ayran and onions with sumach.

Offal

'O truest of true hearts, O Lord from Tebriz, Şems, hundreds of livers have been roasted for you, where is the attraction of yufka bread now?' DI:319-C:2949

Liver with Chick Peas, Onions and Butter

Liver Kalye

'Be so good as to offer the master of the heart a kalye made of that liver blood that, smelling so sweetly and fragrantly of love, nourishes him.' DI:306-C:2823

In the era when this dish was cooked for hours over a brazier fire the chick peas were put in raw. Nowadays we also add tomato puree, tomatoes and tarragon.

Serves 4

- 75g or ½ cup boiled chick peas
- ½ kg or 1lb 2oz mutton or lamb's liver (cut into small chunks)
- 1 tbsp clarified butter
- 1 tbsp sheep's-tail fat
- 1 onion, chopped
- 3 tsp finely chopped fresh mint
- Salt to taste
- 400ml or 1 ¾ cups hot water
- 1 bunch koruk (unripe grapes) the size of a pear or 1 tbsp verjuice to taste

Melt the fat in a frying pan, add the liver and fry. Add the chopped onions and cook until they are golden brown. Put the chick peas in a saucepan and arrange the liver chunks on top. Add the mint and sprinkle with salt. Pour the water over it and add the grapes or grape juice. Cover.

When it starts to boil turn the heat down to low and cook for approx 40–50 minutes. Remove the grapes and arrange the liver on a dish. Serve with bulgur pilav (see p. 81) and sirkencübin (see p. 49) or ayran (see p. 145).

Sheep's Trotters

Paça

'I don't eat sheep's head, it's indigestible; nor sheep's trotters either, they're nothing but bone.' D5:233-C:2695

Paça is a very popular dish; it is also eaten with tandır bread as tirit . Nowadays we sprinkle cayenne pepper over the top.

Serves 4
Cooking time: 3 hours (or 1 hour in a pressure cooker)
— 8 cleaned sheep's trotters
— 2 litres or 8 ⅓ cups water
— 1 tsp salt

For the sauce
— 100ml or ½ cup wine vinegar
— 6 cloves garlic

— ½ tsp salt
— 2 tbsps clarified butter
— ½ tsp cumin
— Tandır bread (see p. 139)

Wash the trotters and put them on to heat with the water. Cook for approximately three hours (one hour in a pressure cooker), until the meat comes away from the bone. Add salt and cook for another 10 minutes. Adding salt before the meat is cooked hardens the tendons and makes the meat tough.

Put the vinegar in a bowl. Pound the garlic thoroughly with the salt and beat it with the vinegar. Pour it into the pan with the boiling trotters. Bring to the boil twice, remove from heat and place in a deep dish.

Heat the clarified butter and pour it over the trotters, sprinkle with cumin and serve accompanied with tandır bread.

Poultry and Game

'Helva, roasted birds; food from the heavens was spread out in abundance, and richly laden tables set.' D:351-C:2662

'My white falcon, the sultan hunts me.
How does the spider revolve around me and spin its web?' 2:395

'The falcon too brings prey from the hills; but gliding with its own wings it is hunted; the sultan therefore keeps it with the partridge and the hazel grouse.' M6:700-C:4678

'Go to the front door, tell Kaymaz to bring the yufka bread and the goose.' M2:329-C:2189

Both Mevlana and many Seljuk references mention the fact that several types of poultry and game were eaten. Partridge and quail were quite common until the 1950s. Today the most frequently used poultry is chicken and cockerel. Konya housewives will not make pilav if there is no chicken stock available. As far as game is concerned, partridge, quail and rabbit are still served in the houses of hunting enthusiasts.

Pilav with Quail

'Speak not of the town, in the desert you have Moses as a travelling companion, you have quail, you have manna.'
5:230-C:2671

According to Ayşe Tırıs, whom I met in Konya in 1979, 'You serve guests who arrive in the evening with pastry cooked in a round copper tray, in the middle of which there will be very hot, spicy arabaşı soup3 made from neck of lamb, chicken or game birds like partridge or quail.' As can be seen from this, poultry and game are used for soup, as well as pilav and stews.

Serves 4

— 4 quails
— 1 litre or 4 cups water
— 1 tsp salt
— 300g or 1 ½ cups long-grain rice
— 600ml or 2 ½ cups warm water and 1 tbsp salt (to soak the rice)
— 400ml or 1 ¾ cups quail stock
— 1 tsp salt
— 150g or ⅔ cup clarified butter
— 150g or ⅔ cup clarified butter (for frying)

Pluck, clean and wash the quails and put them on to heat in a saucepan with the water. When it begins to boil, skim off the foam that forms on the top, cover and cook on a medium heat for approximately one hour, until the quails are tender. Add the salt and remove from the heat after 10 minutes. Strain the quails, reserving the water.

Soak the rice in the warm salty water until the water has cooled. Wash the rice in several changes of water until the water runs clear and drain.

Boil the quail stock with salt. When it comes to a boil add the rice, cover and cook for 3 minutes on a high heat, 3 minutes on medium heat and 10 minutes on a low heat, until the water has been absorbed. Heat 150g fat in a pan and pour over the rice. Turn the heat down to very low. Cover with greased paper and a lid. Allow to cook on a very low heat for 20 minutes. Spoon into a dish.

Heat the remaining fat in a pan, fry the quails, turning them over, arrange on top of the pilav and serve.

Seafood

It is likely that in Mevlana's time fish caught in Lakes Beyşehir and Seydişehir was eaten.

Baked Carp

Mevlana's works refer to shops that prepare foods such as oven roasts, roasted sheep's head and trotters. We can assume that in the Konya of that era carp was prepared in the oven.

Until the 1950s houses in Konya did not have ovens. Dishes that needed to be baked were prepared in large trays and sent to the local bread and simit (savoury roll covered with sesame seeds) bakeries, from where they returned deliciously browned.

When anyone spoke of fish in the 1950s in Konya, the following recipe, sent to the bakery in a baking tin, came to mind. Today we add ½ kilo of potatoes and a tablespoon of tomato puree

Serves 5 or more

— 1kg or 2 ¼ lb carp
— 200ml or 1 cup wine vinegar
— 5 onions, peeled and cut into rings
— 2 heads of garlic, peeled
— 100ml or ½ cup wine vinegar
— Salt to taste
— 200ml or ¾ cup water
— 250g or 1 generous cup clarified butter

Gut and scale the fish. Either leave it whole or divide it into pieces. Wash and drain it. Marinate the fish in 200ml vinegar for one hour. Grease the baking tin with half of the clarified butter. Mix all the other ingredients together in a bowl, add the fish, mix again and place in the greased baking tin. Preheat the oven to 200°C, bake the carp for 30–40 minutes and serve in its tin.

Pulses and Cereals

The lentils and grains of bulgur found at Çatalhöyük show that bulgur and lentils were used in Konya 7000 years ago. We can safely assume that the dishes found in this section were prepared 7000 years ago using the same ingredients. The pulses and cereals, and particularly the chick peas that Mevlana refers to in the thirteenth century, are foods prepared very frequently in Konya by those in the middle income bracket. In Anatolia and Konya chick peas are boiled with meat and kept handy so that a few can be added to any meal as required. Chick peas are such an important part of Adana cuisine that they are even found in dolmas (stuffed vegetables or meat).

Bulgur Wheat with Onions and Meat

Bulgur Aş

'This is war, not a meal of bulgur aş, where you need only roll up your sleeves and start eating.' M5:568-C:3777

'This is not a meal of bulgur aş, come and behold this sword: we need Hamza[4] to make this line of soldiers resist like metal.' M5:569-C:3778

Today when we prepare this recipe we fry three or four green peppers along with the onions. After the bulgur has been fried we also add tomato puree or fresh tomatoes.

Serves 4

— 2 tbsps clarified butter (see glossary)
— 1 onion, finely chopped
— 300g or 1 ½ cups bulgur wheat
— 150g or 1 ½ cups lamb kavurma (see p. 161)
— 1 litre or 4 cups hot meat stock

Fry the onions in the clarified butter. Add the bulgur and continue to fry. Add the kavurma and meat stock and cover. When it begins to boil, lower the heat. Cook for 20–25 minutes, until the bulgur becomes soft. Pour into a dish and serve.

Chopped Meat with Wheat

Herise (Keşkek)

'One day a child was at home alone and felt a sudden urge to eat herise. I want some herise, he said. A bowl of herise appeared from thin air. The child ate his fill. When his mother and father returned he told them what had happened. His father said Praise God that you have reached such an exalted position and that your faith and trust in God has been strengthened.' F:266

Herise is a Seljuk dish mentioned in Mevlana's works and in the Histories of the Seljuks. In many parts of Anatolia it is served at weddings and functions. It is rarely prepared in Konya today.

Serves 5 or more

— 300g or 3 cups döğme (dehusked wheat)
— 1 neck of lamb or whole chicken
— 2 litres or 8 ⅓ cups water
— 2 tbsps clarified butter
— 3 onions, finely chopped 1 tsp cumin
— Salt to taste
— 4 tbsp butter and ½ tsp cumin, to garnish

Pick over the dehusked wheat, wash and soak overnight in water. In the morning wash the chicken or the chuck and place in a saucepan together with the dehusked wheat and water. Cook on a medium heat until both the meat and the wheat are completely tender. Remove the meat, shred it without allowing it to cool and return it to the saucepan. In a separate pan fry the onions in the clarified butter, stir in the cumin and add to the boiling soup.

Crush the wheat with a wooden ladle until it is the consistency of thick set yogurt. Transfer to a shallow pan, heat the butter, pour it over the top, sprinkle with cumin and serve.

Pilav with Bulgur

Lentil Aş

'I've eaten neither kavurma, nor tirit, nor lentils ...
Just tell me what you have eaten and drunk, that will do.'
M6:120-C:722

Anatolian cuisine boasts a rich selection of aş (hot cooked dishes). As is shown here, there are different varieties of lentil aş, with bulgur and home made pasta. Other pulses can also be used for making aş.

Serves 4 or more

- 60g or 4 ½ tbsp clarified butter
- 1 tsp sheep's-tail fat
- 1 chopped onion
- 100g or ½ cup lamb, chopped using the bıçak arası technique (see glossary)
- 800ml or 3 ⅓ cups meat stock
- 150g or ⅔ cup lentils
- 75g or ⅓ cup bulgur wheat
- ½ tsp black pepper
- Salt to taste
- 1 tsp dried mint

Fry the onion in the fat. Add the chopped meat and fry until it has absorbed all the juices it has released. Add the meat stock. When it comes to a boil add the lentils. When the lentils are half cooked, add the bulgur wheat and the black pepper. Cook for approximately 40-50 minutes, until the lentils are tender. Remove from heat, sprinkle with the dried mint, ladle into bowls and serve.

Pilav with Erişte (Homemade Pasta)

Lentil Aş

'My tears, muddied with grief, have made their mark. The outcome: my face no longer endures sullenness, nor my bowl base lentil aş.'

4:392-C:3771

This dish is very popular in many other parts of Anatolia, as well as Konya. It is either poured over tandır bread and eaten as tirit or prepared with a higher proportion of water and eaten as soup.

Serves 5 or more

— 150g or ⅔ cup brown or green lentils
— 800ml or 3 ⅓ cups water for boiling
— 250g or 1 cup meat kavurma (see p. 161)
— 5 onions, finely chopped
— 1 litre or 4 cups meat stock or water
— Salt to taste
— 150g or 1 cup erişte (see p. 205)
— 1 tsp cumin

— 1 tsp mint
— 2 portions yogurt with garlic (see Yogurt with Garlic, p. 101)
— 125g or ½ cup clarified butter or butter, to garnish

Boil the lentils for approximately 15–20 minutes, until half-cooked. Strain. Place the kavurma and onions in a saucepan and cook until the onions turn golden brown. Add the hot meat stock, the lentils and the salt. When it begins to boil, add the erişte and sprinkle the cumin and mint over it. Cook for 20–30 minutes, until it has thickened.

Prepare the yogurt with garlic. Take a ladleful of warm liquid and mix it into the yogurt, then add the yogurt a little at a time to the saucepan. Ladle into a deep dish. Heat the butter, pour over the top and serve.

Chick Pea Stew

Nohutlu Yahni

'No sooner does the saucepan boil than the chick peas start leaping up to the top, in hundreds of manifestations of ecstasy.'

M3:481-C:4161

Nohutlu yahni must have been one of the principal dishes of that era. The Turks who adopted Anatolia as their home did not take long to start adding the pulses widely produced there, such as chick peas, beans and black-eyed peas, to their boiled meat dishes. In some towns in the Aegean and Marmara regions nohutlu yahni is served at wedding feasts, along with herise.

Onion rings can also be added to this dish. White kidney bean yahni (stew) is prepared in exactly the same way, using white kidney beans instead of chick peas.

Serves 4
- 150g or ½ cup chick peas soaked overnight in water
- ½ kg or 1lb 2oz bony lamb
- 2 peeled onions
- litre or 4 cups water
- Salt to taste

Wash the chick peas and meat and place in a saucepan together with the onion. Add the water and put on to heat. When it comes to the boil, skim off the foam that forms on the top, cover and cook for 70–80 minutes on a low heat until the meat and chick peas are tender. Add salt and cook for another five minutes, then remove from heat. Remove the onions, ladle the stew into a serving dish together with the accompanying liquid and serve.

Vegetable Dishes

The vegetables mentioned in Mevlana's works are cowpeas, beans, carrots, cucumbers, spinach, marrows, cabbage, lettuce, celery, leeks, garlic, onions, radishes and turnips. For this reason this section contains only recipes using those vegetables. As you will see, all the dishes in this section call for animal fat. There are no vegetable dishes prepared with olive oil because we know from Mevlana's works that olive oil was used as fuel in oil lamps.

Fresh Cowpeas with Yogurt and Rice

Fresh Cowpea Borani

'There where there are beans and cowpeas,
your sugar cane sprouts in springtime.' D3:171-C:1518

In Konya we make borani with green beans and, in spring, with broad beans when they first come into season.

Serves 4

— ½ kg or 1lb 2oz fresh cowpeas or green beans
— 200ml or 1 cup water
— ¼ tsp salt
— tbsps clarified butter
— portion yogurt with garlic (see Yogurt with Garlic, p. 101)
— tbsps clarified butter, to garnish

Trim the cowpeas, wash and snap them into two or three pieces each, by hand. Add them to the boiling salted water. Cook them for approximately 30 minutes, until tender. Strain.

Heat the clarified butter in a pan, add the cowpeas and stir for 3–4 minutes, until well coated with the butter. Mix them into the yogurt with garlic and arrange on a plate. Heat the clarified butter, pour over the top and serve hot.

Sour Spinach

'I am your spinach; cook me as you desire, sour or sweet.'

MI:437-C:2418

Sour spinach is a very common dish, although now it is made with lemons.

Serves 4

— ½ kg or 1lb 2oz spinach
— 250g or 1 generous cup lamb, chopped using the bıçak arası technique (see glossary)
— 2 tbsp clarified butter
— 1 onion, finely chopped
— 600ml or 2 ½ cups hot water
— Salt to taste
— 40g or ¼ cup bulgur wheat or rice
— Verjuice or sour pomegranate juice to taste
— Tandır bread (see p. 139)

Wash the spinach carefully and drain. Put the meat in a saucepan and fry until it has reabsorbed all the juices it has released. Add the clarified butter and the onions and fry until they have turned golden brown. Add the water and cook for 30–40 minutes, until the meat is tender. Add the spinach, salt, bulgur wheat or rice, cover and cook on a low heat for another 10–15 minutes. Before removing from heat pour the verjuice over the top. Bring to the boil twice more. Allow to stand for 10 minutes, transfer to a dish and serve accompanied with tandır bread.

Butternut Squash (Sour Squash)

'My beauty made a face and brought down the price of sugar, reduced its value; who knows what wine my beloved has in that sour pumpkin.'

D3:216-C:208

Who can say whether Mevlana was not referring to Konya's sour butternut squash dish in the above couplet? Sour butternut squash is the most popular dish in Konya. Old ladies in Konya advocate that it should be eaten the day after it has been prepared. According to them, before there were refrigerators, food left in the garden covered with a *sele* (a flat wicker basket used for drying mint, laying out börek before frying, etc) reposed overnight watching the moon and stars, acquired a golden colour and improved in flavour.

This dish may also be prepared in the same way as it is today, by adding four peeled tomatoes. If verjuice is unavailable you can use lemon juice, as we now do. Moreover, if you do not want the herbs to be visible you can put them in whole and remove them before serving.

If you are not cooking on a brazier you can parboil the meat and chick peas before adding them to the other ingredients. That way you will ensure that the meat and chick peas will not be tough.

Serves 4

— ½ kg or 1lb 2oz fatty mutton ribs (divided into hand sized pieces)
— 75g or ½ cup chick peas
— 2 tbsp clarified butter or sheep's-tail fat

- 3 onions, finely chopped
- 1 head of garlic, divided into 2 or 3 pieces
- Pinch of chopped marigold leaves
- Pinch of chopped sweet basil
- 5 tbsps chopped fresh or dried mint
- 1 butternut squash, 1–1.5 kg, peeled and cut into triangles
- 100ml or ½ cup verjuice
- 100ml or ½ cup water
- Salt to taste

Arrange the fat, chick peas and meat in a saucepan in layers. Place the onions, basil, marigold leaves and mint on top. Add the pumpkin in layers. Pour on the verjuice and water and add salt. Cover and cook. When it comes to the boil turn the heat down to very low. Cook for about 90 minutes, until the meat and chick peas are tender. Reheat the following day, spoon into a dish and serve.

Spinach with Onions

Spinach Borani

'Just before daybreak I heard an excited voice; the lovely aroma of kalye and borani is wafting towards me.' D4:120-C:1059

Borani is an Eastern dish. According to legend it got its name from the colour and scene on the pearl-embroidered green rug in the trousseau of the Caliph Memnun's wife, Boranduht. Although it is prepared with all vegetables, in Anatolia the variety best befitting the legend is with rice and spinach. In

Konya bulgur wheat is often used in borani too. You can leave the rice and bulgur out, if you wish.

Borani can also be prepared with meat, in which case the spinach is cooked without the verjuice. The borani is then blended with yogurt with garlic and hot fat poured over the top. My favourite version is the one below.

Serves 4

— ½ kg or 1lb 2oz spinach
— 200ml or 1 cup water and ½ tsp salt (for boiling the spinach)
— 1 tbsp clarified butter
— 1 onion, finely chopped
— 400ml or 2 cups hot meat stock
— Salt to taste
— 75g or ⅓ cup rice or bulgur
— 1 portion yogurt with garlic (see p. 101)
— 125g or ½ cup butter, to garnish
— Tandır bread (see p. 139)

Trim, wash and chop the spinach. Heat the water for boiling, add the spinach, boil for 5 minutes, strain.

Put the clarified butter in a saucepan, add the onions and cook until they are golden brown. Add the meat stock, salt, parboiled spinach and rice or bulgur wheat. When it comes to a boil turn the heat down to very low and cook for 15–20 minutes, until the rice has softened. Leave to stand for 10 minutes. When it has cooled slightly, mix with the yogurt with garlic. Transfer to a dish, heat the butter, drizzle over the top and serve with tandır bread.

Cabbage Borani

'To the cucumber field, the cabbage field, the onion field, or to a rose garden?' FM:169

Cabbage kapıska (a kind of sauerkraut made with fried onions, pickled cabbage and rice) is made with the leftover pieces of cabbage in every house in Konya where cabbage dolma has been prepared. Nowadays we add tomato paste to the meat and onions as they are frying and because chilli goes very well with cabbage, we also add hot red pepper flakes. If it is not prepared as borani with garlic and yogurt, it is eaten as kapıska, with a generous squeeze of lemon juice.

Serves 4

— ½ kg or 1lb 2oz cabbage, or the hard part in the heart of the cabbage
— 1 tbsp clarified butter
— 1 onion, finely chopped
— 250g or 1 generous cup fatty mutton, chopped according to the bıçak arası technique (see glossary)
— 400ml or 2 cups meat stock
— Salt to taste
— 75g or ⅓ cup bulgur wheat or rice
— 1 serving yogurt with garlic (see p. 101)
— 60g or 5 tbsps clarified butter (see glossary), to garnish

Break off the cabbage leaves and wash them, or, with a meat cleaver, finely chop the hard centre of the cabbage left over from making dolma.

Put the chopped meat into a saucepan. Put it on to heat and fry until the meat has reabsorbed all the juices it releases; add the onions and fry until they have turned golden brown. Add the cabbage leaves and stir briefly. Add the meat stock, salt and bulgur wheat or rice. Cook on a low heat for 30–40 minutes. Allow to stand for 10 minutes. Mix in the yogurt with garlic gradually, transfer to a copper dish and serve.

Sweet Spinach

Sweet spinach no longer exists in present-day Konya. But it's likely that during that era it was prepared in the same way as Konya's famous courgette dish. As it is mentioned by Mevlana, I couldn't resist including it.

Serves 4

— 250g or 9 oz fatty lamb ribs divided into 4 pieces
— 2 tbsps chick peas, soaked overnight
— 600ml or 2 ½ cups water
— Salt to taste
— ½ kg or 1lb 2oz spinach
— 1 tbsp clarified butter
— 50ml or ¼ cup of wine vinegar
— 125g or ½ cup of grape syrup (pekmez)

Boil the meat and chick peas in the water for approximately 30 minutes until tender. Add salt and cook for another 5 minutes. Reserve 200ml water and discard the rest. Trim, wash and strain the spinach, then add to the saucepan. Add the clarified butter, vinegar and grape syrup; cook on a low heat for 10–15 minutes, until the spinach is soft. Transfer to a dish and serve with tandır bread.

Celery with Meat and Onions

Celery Kalye

'They recognised and knew, as well as if they were distinguishing a rose from celery, each hair, each particle of the composition of the self.' M1:133-C:370

Nowadays in Konya we prepare celery with olive oil and a sauce. The sauce is made without koruk (unripe grapes). We add two egg yolks beaten with 50ml lemon juice to the cooked dish, which is brought to the boil once and removed from the heat.

Serves 4

- 250g or 9oz mutton or lamb ribs, divided into 4 pieces
- 2 tbsps clarified butter
- 1 onion, finely chopped
- ½ kg or 1lb 2oz celery
- 600ml or 2 ½ cups hot meat stock
- Salt to taste
- A bunch of koruk (unripe grapes) – the size of a pear – or 1 tbsp verjuice to taste

Wash the meat, place in a saucepan and put on to heat. When it has reabsorbed all the juices it has released add the clarified butter and onions and fry until the onions have turned light brown. Bring the meat together in a pile in the centre of the saucepan. Trim and wash the celery and chop it into slices. Add it to the saucepan, beginning by placing it around the meat. Add the meat stock and salt and cover. When it begins to boil, add the koruk or verjuice. Cook on a low heat for 40–50 minutes until the celery has softened and drain, reserving the liquid. Tip the contents of the saucepan into a dish by placing the dish over the saucepan and turning upside-down. Add the reserved drained liquid and serve.

Courgettes

'It is a bizarre tree, to sometimes yield apples, sometimes pumpkins, at times poison, at times sugar, now it grows sorrow, and later strength.' DI:15-C:95

It is highly likely that pumpkin kalye and the courgette dish we make today were originally the same thing. Burhan Oğuz says, 'Kalle pumpkin is Konya's courgette dish; in Konya, galle is the name given to a dish made from stewed sweet and red pumpkins.' In Konya milky pumpkin pudding is called pumpkin galle (galle gabak). According to the ladies of Konya, this dish does not need any additional fat, as it is made with fatty meat. There are no onions either, because it contains pekmez.

If you are not cooking on a brazier you should parboil the meat and chick peas before adding them to the other ingredients to make sure they do not remain hard.

Serves 4

— ½ kg or 1lb 2oz fatty mutton ribs, divided into hand-sized pieces
— 75g or ½ cup chick peas
— ½ kg or 1lb 2oz courgettes
— 1 tbsp clarified butter
— 50ml or ¼ cup vinegar
— 3 tbsps pekmez (grape syrup)
— 200ml or ¾ cup water
— Salt to taste

Wash the meat and place in a large pot. Wash the chick peas and scatter them over the meat. Wash the courgettes, cut them into slices and arrange them on top of the meat. Add the clarified butter, vinegar, pekmez, water and salt and cover. When it begins to boil, turn the heat down to low and cook for approximately 60 minutes, until the meat becomes tender.

Leeks with Meat and Onions

Leek Kalye

'The ears of corn are swaying in the dawn breeze,
the plains overflow with bright green leeks.' M4:445-C:3251

In Konya, leeks are used a great deal in winter. Nowadays we prepare them with tomato puree and chilli flakes, which go well with the leeks. We do not use cinnamon. It is likely that the cinnamon added to leeks in Ottoman cuisine came from the Seljuk era.

Serves 4

— ½ kg or 1lb 2oz leeks
— 250g or 1 generous cup lamb or mutton, cut into small chunks 1 tbsp clarified butter
— 1 tsp clarified sheep's-tail fat
— 1 onion, finely chopped
— 200ml or 1 cup meat stock (see p. 52)
— ½ tsp cinnamon
— Salt to taste
— 1 bunch of koruk – the size of a pear – or 1 tbsp verjuice to taste

Trim the leeks and chop them into 4cm pieces, wash and drain them in a sieve. Put the meat in a saucepan and fry until it has reabsorbed all the juices it has released. Add the clarified butter, the sheep's-tail fat and the onions and fry until the onions have turned light brown.

Place the leeks on top and add the meat stock. Add the cinnamon and salt and cover. When it begins to boil turn the heat down to low. Add the unripe grapes or verjuice. Cook for approximately 40–50 minutes, until the meat and leeks are tender.

Turnip Kalye

'Is it not ridiculous to cook turnip in a gold saucepan?' FM:25

Turnip is rarely used in Konya. The couplet above shows that it was a lowly vegetable in that era too. In Konya there is a belief that turnip has healing powers. It is said, 'Even if you don't eat turnip you should definitely walk through a turnip field once a year.' When we cook turnips we add cayenne pepper and tomato puree.

Serves 4

- 250g or 1 generous cup lamb or mutton, cut into small chunks
- 1 onion, finely chopped
- 1 tsp sheep's-tail fat
- 1 tsp clarified butter
- ½ kg or 1lb 2oz turnip
- 600ml or 2 ½ cups hot water
- Salt to taste

Wash the meat and place in a saucepan. Fry until it has absorbed all the juices it has released. Add the fats and the onions and fry them until they have become light brown. While the meat is frying peel the turnips and cut them into round slices. Wash and drain them, then add them to the fried meat. Stir once or twice. Add the water and salt and cover. When the water boils, turn the heat to low. Cook for approximately one hour, until all the liquid has been absorbed. Transfer to a dish and serve with bulgur pilav.

Dishes with Fruit

The fruits Mevlana mentions in his works are pears, quinces, mulberries, apples, plums, dates, figs, water melons, melons, carob, pomegranates, peaches, Seville oranges, grapes and apricots.

Stewed Quince with Pekmez

'Anything boiled in pekmez acquires its flavour.
Carrots, apples, quinces, walnuts. Boil what you will, it will give you the flavour of pekmez.' M5:391-C:2487–8

Fruit dishes with pekmez are typical in Konya. Because they are prepared with sugar nowadays I have included the measurements for sugar. Mevlana did not mention it but it is likely that the delicious squash, aubergine, quince and apricot jams of present-day Konya made with pekmez came from that era.

Serves 4

— ½ kg or 1lb 2oz quince
— 400ml or 1 ¾ cups water
— 2 tbsps clarified butter or butter
— 2 tbsps rice
— 150g or ⅔ cup of sugar or pekmez (grape syrup)

Wash, peel, core and slice the quinces and place in a saucepan. Add the water and cover. Cook on a low heat for approximately 25–30 minutes, until the quinces become soft. Add the butter and rice. When the rice has cooked, after 15–20 minutes, add the sugar or pekmez. Remove from heat when all the liquid has been absorbed. Leave to repose in the pan for 10 minutes. Transfer to a porcelain dish and serve hot.

Apples with Pekmez

'God, who is free from all deficiency, creates an apple orchard,
He hides the apples of meaning among branches of letters, leaves of words.
The smell of apples wafts out of that sheet of words, that noise
resembling branches and leaves, only He remains unseen.
Inhale this fragrance, inhale it well that it may envelop you, draw you
back to your origins.' M6:12-C:84,85,86

Serves 4
— ½ kg or 1lb 2oz apples
— 400ml or 1 ¾ cups water
— 2 tbsps clarified butter or butter
— 2 tbsps rice
— 75g or ⅓ cup sugar or 250g or 1 cup pekmez (grape syrup)

Wash, peel, core and slice the apples. Place in a saucepan. Add the water and cover. Cook on a low heat for approximately 15–20 minutes, until the apples are soft. Add the clarified butter and rice. After 15–20 minutes, when the rice is cooked, pour in the sugar or pekmez. After 5–10 minutes, when all the liquid has been absorbed, remove from the heat. Leave to repose in the pan for 10 minutes. Transfer to a porcelain dish and serve hot.

Carrots with Pekmez

Serves 4

— ½ kg or 1lb 2oz carrots
— 400ml or 1 ¾ cups water
— 2 tbsps clarified butter or butter
— 2 tbsps rice
— 150g or ⅔ cup sugar or pekmez (grape syrup)

Wash, peel and slice the carrots and arrange them in layers in a saucepan. Add the water and cover. Cook on a low heat for approximately 30 minutes, until the carrots are soft. Add the clarified butter and the rice. After 15–20 minutes, when the rice has cooked, pour in the sugar or pekmez. Remove from heat after 5–10 minutes, when all the liquid has been absorbed. Leave in the pan to repose for 10 minutes. Transfer to a porcelain dish and serve hot.

Salads

Yogurt and Cucumber Salad

Cacık

It is mentioned in *The Book of the Wise* that Mevlana ate, and was fond of, yogurt with garlic. The fact that cucumber was available in Anatolia in that era is an indication that cacık originates from that time.

Serves 4–6

— 1 portion yogurt with garlic (see below)
— Water
— 2 cucumbers
— 1 tbsp chopped fresh mint or ½ tsp dried mint

Prepare the yogurt with garlic and dilute to the consistency you desire. Peel the cucumbers and chop them into tiny cubes. Mix with the yogurt and sprinkle with the mint.

Yogurt with Garlic

'Once again the esteemed imam of the great tomb,
Hazreti Bahaeddin-i Bahri relates the following legend:

Mevlana and I went to a hot spring in Ilgin together.
Mevlana sat in the hot spring for exactly ten days without eating anything.
Suddenly a Turk brought a large bowl of yogurt.
Mevlana added quite a large quantity of garlic to it and ate it.
After that he occupied himself with the sema for forty days
and ate nothing at all.'
Eflaki, *The Book of the Wise 1*, p:316

In the same work Kerra Hatun also relates that Mevlana added chopped garlic to sour yogurt.

My recipe for yogurt with garlic calls for strained yogurt from Konya. Strained yogurt has a consistency similar to that of curd cheese and it is delicious. As well as being used in many famous restaurants in Anatolia, the yogurt of Konya is also proudly offered in the restaurants of big cities like Istanbul and Ankara. You can achieve a similar consistency by straining thick set yogurt through cheesecloth or muslin overnight. Strained yogurt is excellent with mantı (homemade stuffed pasta served with yogurt), tutmaç (pasta with meat and yogurt), yogurt soup and cacık.

If you prefer a more liquid yogurt with garlic you can blend it with more water.

— 250g or 1 cup Konya thick set yogurt
— 100ml or ½ cup water
— 2 cloves garlic
— Salt to taste

Mix the yogurt with the water. Peel the garlic and grind it with the salt. Mix with the yogurt and use as required.

Chopped Onions with Parsley and Sumac

Onion Piyaz with Sumac

As Mevlana mentions sumac and onions in his works it is probable that onion piyaz with sumach, which is a typical side dish in Konya homes and restaurants, dates back to that era. Onion piyaz with sumac is served with every type of köfte and kebab. We can also add chopped parsley to it. In restaurants, the onions are chopped and sumac is added to them before they are 'killed' with salt.

Serves 4

— 4 onions

— 1 tsp salt
— 1 tsp sumac

Cut the onions into very thin slices. Sprinkle with salt and set aside for three minutes. Rub the salt in by hand, wash and squeeze out the excess moisture. Mix with the sumac and serve.

Pilav and Pasta

Although Mevlana talks about rice in his works there is no mention of the name 'pilav'. But this is what Sultan Veled says about dishes prepared with rice:

Good or poor, thick or fine fabrics, satins and silks of every shade,
Different dishes from every land, made with rice, prepared with kebab,
There are sour, sweet, red, yellow, white dishes offered to every guest,
These are things desired by the sheep-like masses,
consider it all as having come from the ground.
If there is a hint of enlightenment in you, then consider that born of soil, that which is soil, as soil.

İbtida-Name, p:35

'Dishes made with rice' doubtless refers to pilav. In Seljuk references pilav goes under the name of 'dane', while Eflaki calls it pilav.

I am therefore including the recipes for bulgur and plain pilav here. As far as pasta is concerned, it is likely that the erişte (homemade pasta) used in tutmaç soup (see Tutmaç Soup, p. 58) was cooked in the same way as pilav. Besides, in Konya erişte is referred to as 'erişte pilav'. It is likely that in that era, as in Konya until recently, pilav was prepared using the stewing method (i.e. rice is added to boiling stock, rather than boiling stock added to rice that has first been fried in butter). For this reason I have used the stewing method for all my pilav recipes.

Bulgur Pilav

Bulgur pilav is widely prepared in Konya and Anatolia. As well as the plain bulgur pilav below, in Konya bulgur pilav is also prepared by frying oil, onions, tomato puree and then adding meat stock and bulgur. It is delicious. Pilav prepared with sheep's head is also a real delicacy. If sheep's head is unavailable, the old ladies of Konya advise adding a spoonful of clarified sheep's-tail fat to the bulgur pilav to obtain a similar flavour (see Kelle Kebab or Sheep's-Head Kebab, p. 155).

Serves 4

— 600ml or 2 ½ cups meat stock (see p. 52)
— ½ tsp salt
— 300g or 1 ½ cups bulgur wheat
— 200g or 1 cup clarified butter
— Yogurt or ayran (see p. 145)

Boil the meat stock with the salt. Add the bulgur wheat and cover. Cook on high heat for 3 minutes and medium heat for 5 minutes, then on a low heat until the bulgur has absorbed all the water and formed small craters. Heat the clarified butter in a frying pan and drizzle over the top, then turn down the heat to very low and allow to steep for 20 minutes. Transfer to a dish and serve with yogurt or ayran.

Rice Pilav

Serves 4

— 300g or 1 ½ cups long grain rice
— 1 tbsp salt and 400ml or 1 ¾ cups warm water (for soaking the rice)
— 400ml or 1 ¾ cups meat or chicken stock
— 1 tsp salt
— 150g or ⅔ cup clarified butter or butter

Pick over the rice. Place in a bowl, cover completely with salted warm waterand soak until the water has cooled. Wash in several changes of water until the water runs clear. Drain. Place the meat or chicken stock into a saucepan, add the salt. Once it comes to a boil, add the rice and cover. When it begins to boil again, cook for 3 minutes on a high heat, 3 minutes on a medium heat and approximately 10 minutes on a low heat, until it has absorbed all the liquid and formed small craters. Heat the clarified butter in a frying pan and drizzle over the top. Cover with greased paper and a lid and allow to steep on a very low heat for 20 minutes. You can also use a heat diffuser.

Homemade Pasta with Mint

Tatar Aşı

'You have boiled and burned with fervour for so long, but o withered dried soul, like Tatar aşı, you are still half raw.' M6:275-C:1780

Tatar aşı is prepared as set out below. However if you cut the dough into smaller squares and prepare the yogurt to soup consistency it is known as 'kesme soup with pastry croûtons'. Both are delicious.

If you do not prepare pastry croûtons, reserve one piece of dough and cut it into fine strips. These strips can be fried and used to garnish the tatar aşı.

Serves 4

For the dough
— 100g or 1 cup strong plain flour
— 1 egg
— 50ml or ¼ cup water
— ½ tsp salt

To boil
— 1 litre or 1 ¾ pints meat stock or water
— ½ tsp salt

To sprinkle over the dough
— 50ml or ¼ cup water

To coat

— 1 portion yogurt with garlic (see p. 101)

To garnish

— 125g or ½ cup clarified butter or butter
— ½ tsp dried mint
— 1 portion of kikirdek (pastry croûtons) (see Tutmaç Soup, p. 58)

Sieve the flour, make a well in the centre and add the egg, water and salt. Knead until you have a soft, pliable dough. Divide the dough into two pieces, cover with a damp cloth and allow to stand for 30 minutes. With a rolling pin roll out sheets 3mm thick. Cut into 2cm squares and allow to stand on a cloth for 15–20 minutes.

Prepare the pastry croûtons. (See p. 61)

Boil the stock or water with the salt. Add the squares of dough. Boil for 20 minutes, until the dough has softened, remove from heat and sprinkle with the water. Drain after 3–4 minutes, reserving the water.

Prepare the yogurt with garlic using the hot drained water from the pasta; mix the pasta with the yogurt and place into a large deep dish. Heat the clarified butter and add the mint. Remove from heat before the mint turns black and pour over the pasta. Sprinkle with the pastry croutons and serve while still warm.

Börek

'I want tutmaç, I want börek, I want helva, I want dates.' FM:13

'A poor man on the road stopped at the house of a noble man and became his guest. The owner of the mansion lavished all the attentions of hospitality and generosity on him. He placed sumptuous kebabs before him, böreks never seen before, lit candles in his assembly room, summoned beauties for him, and clothed him with fine outfits.' DI:379-C:3479–80

Although in Mevlana's works börek is referred to in the plural as 'böreks never seen before', no mention is made of any particular börek. Given that he writes about yufka bread, it is likely that saç börek and other böreks made with rolled out pastry, prepared with the same dough and in the same way, were amongst these 'never seen before' böreks. As he mentions tandır bread it is also likely that tandır börek, made by adding a filling to the same dough, dates back to that era. As he mentions loaves of bread baked in local bakeries, it is likely that the cheese böreks known as çarşı (shop-bought) börek were also prepared there because these böreks, which are an integral part of Konya cuisine, have been served at traditional functions for centuries. I believe that su (water) börek needs to be included here too, because the fact that dishes such as mantı (homemade pasta served with yogurt), tatar aş and tutmaç, where the dough is boiled, were prepared in that era makes it likely that su börek also dates back to that time.

Börek Fillings

These fillings can be used in any börek of your choice. Today fresh parsley has taken the place of mint – we do not use dried parsley. If you are going to use dried herbs, use dried mint.

Spinach Filling

— ½ kg or 1lb 2oz spinach
— 2 onions
— 2 tbsps clarified butter (if you are going to fry the onions first)
— 250g or 1 generous cup of diced meat or minced meat kavurma (see p. 161) or crumbled feta cheese
— Salt and black pepper to taste

The ingredients can either be chopped and mixed together raw, or cooked as follows. Fry the onions in the clarified butter, add the meat and stir. Now add the spinach and stir again, then add the seasoning. If you are using cheese, fry the onions in the clarified butter, add the spinach and stir. Season and remove from heat, then mix in the cheese.

Cartilage Filling

— 250g or 9oz cartilage (sheep's-tail with the fat removed by clarifying)
— 2 onions, finely chopped
— 6 tbsp chopped fresh mint, or dried mint to taste
— Salt and black pepper to taste

Place all the ingredients in a bowl and mix well.

Minced Meat Filling

— 250g or 1 generous cup of lamb, chopped very finely
— bıçak arası (see glossary)
— 2 onions, finely chopped
— 6 tbsps chopped parsley
— Salt and black pepper to taste

Place the meat in a frying pan and put on to heat. When it absorbs the juices it has released, add the onions and fry. Add the black pepper, salt and parsley and remove from heat.

Cheese Filling

— 250g or 1 generous cup of crumbled blue cheese from Konya, or goat's or ewe's cheese encased in a skin, or feta cheese
— 2 onions, finely chopped
— 4 tbsps chopped fresh mint, or dried mint to taste
— Salt to taste (if the cheese is very salty it may not be necessary)
— Black pepper to taste

Place all the ingredients in a bowl and mix well.

Griddled Cheese Börek

Saç Börek

Saç börek is prepared by every housewife in Konya.The pastry for saç börek should be thin enough to read a newspaper through. To stop the pastry from tearing, only very dry cheese and a small amount of filling should be used in preparing this dish. In the past, this börek got its flavour from the thinness of the pastry and the butter obtained from the cow in the back yard, the way saç börek was prepared in the old Sedirler district. Although bought saç börek no longer has these characteristics, it is still very popular with foreigners.

Serves 5 or more

— 100g or 1 cup plain flour
— 100g or 1 cup strong plain flour
— 100g or 1 cup wholemeal flour
— 200ml or 2 cups water
— ½ tsp salt
— 100g or 1 cup plain flour for rolling out the dough
— 1 portion of cheese börek filling (the cheese should be very dry)
— 250g or 1 cup butter

Sift all the flour on to a pastry board. Make a well in the centre, add the water and salt and knead to make a soft, pliable dough. Divide the dough into egg- sized pieces. Allow to stand under a damp cloth for 30 minutes. Roll out the dough in the thinnest sheets possible. Place cheese filling on to half of each piece and fold the other half over into a half moon shape, pressing down the edges with your fingers. Place in a saç or wok, on a very low heat. Cook for 3–4 minutes. When one side is cooked, turn over and cook the other side. Transfer to a metallic tray, brush each börek with the melted butter and pile them on top of each other. Cover with a lid, then wrap in a cloth and allow to stand for 5–10 minutes. Serve in the tray.

Börek Cooked in Water

Su Börek

Su börek is the main börek on the traditional menu in Konya. The taste of homemade su börek in Konya is quite exceptional and I have never come across it in any other region of Turkey. In Konya, su börek is generally made with meat filling. The dough is rolled out very thinly, boiled in water for at least two minutes and cooked thoroughly on a brazier or stove to soften it. When it is cut into slices and picked up, the layers of pastry do not stick together but are flaky and crumbly.

Su börek is the main börek on the menu for important functions in Konya, the *kara yemek* menu, comprising a minimum of three savoury courses and one sweet. Its popularity makes it an indispensable part alongside modern cakes, biscuits, çörek (milk bread) and börek of the afternoon teas that today are an established part of life, quietly and confidently displaying the nobility inherited from the Seljuks. These meals are no longer served on the floor on round copper trays, but laid out on tables.

Serves 5 or more

— A round baking tin 35–40cm in diameter
— 2 tbsps clarified butter, for greasing the tin
— 1 portion of meat börek filling
— 5 eggs
— 100ml or ½ cup water
— 1 tsp salt
— 250g or 2 cups strong plain flour
— 250g or 2 cups self-raising flour
— 1 cup of melted clarified butter, for brushing the dough

— 3 litres or 12 ½ cups water with 2 tbsps salt, for boiling the dough
— 2 tbsps clarified butter, to prevent the dough from sticking

Sift the flour on to a pastry board. Make a well in the centre and break the eggs into it. Add the water and salt, knead into a firm pastry by gathering the flour from the edges. Knead for 15 minutes, divide into 12 pieces of dough and place on a floured tray. Allow to rest under a damp cloth for 30 minutes.

Roll out the pastry with an *oklavı* (a thin, cane-like rolling pin) into the thinnest sheets possible. Sprinkle a tiny amount of flour over each piece and pile them one on top of the other. Reserve two of the most even sheets for the top and bottom of the tray and line the bottom with one piece. Divide all the other pieces into four.

Boil the 3 litres of water in a large saucepan with the salt and 2 tbsps clarified butter. Place the squares of dough in the water two or three pieces at a time and boil for at least 2 minutes. When the dough rises to the surface remove with a perforated ladle and place into a saucepan of cold water. Drain by placing on an upside-down sieve and arrange in the tray in layers. Drizzle a tablespoonful of melted clarified butter over every two or three layers of pastry. When you have arranged half the pieces in this way, distribute the filling evenly over the pastry and continue to arrange the rest of the sheets over the top as before, boiling each piece first for 2 minutes. When you have arranged the last piece, cover with the dry sheet of pastry you have reserved and brush the top with clarified butter. Cook on top of the stove, turning the tray from time to time, or in an oven preheated to 200°C, for 25–30 minutes.

Tandır Börek

Tandır börek is another of Konya's superb böreks. Hazret-i Mevlana may well say, 'Once you have had just one taste of the food of light you will strew earth over bread and tandır alike,'but, for us mere mortals this börek, with its legendary aroma, cooked in the heat of the tandır and split and spread with butter the moment it comes out, is the food of the Gods, and cannot be equalled.

In place of the raising agent given here you may use any of the commercial yeasts available today.

For 6 böreks (cooked in a glowing tandır after the flames have died down or in a conventional oven)

— 1 portion cheese or meat börek filling
— 2 tbsp clarified butter to grease the tin
— 150g or 1 ½ cups plain flour
— 150g or 1 ½ cups strong plain flour
— 150g or 1 ½ cups wholemeal flour
— 2 tbsp raising agent (See Bazlama, p. 137)
— 1 tbsp warm water
— ½ tsp salt
— 300ml or 1 ¼ cups warm water
— Enough clarified butter to brush the böreks
— Ayran (see p. 145) or Apricot Hoşaf (see p. 135) to serve

Sift all the flour on to a pastry board, make a well in the centre and add the raising agent and the tablespoon of water. Mix 1 tsp flour into the raising agent and mound the rest of the flour over it. Wait for the raising agent to work. When cracks appear in the flour, make another well in the centre, add salt and 300ml water and mix to a dough with the consistency of thick set yogurt. Leave it to rise under a damp cloth until it can be stretched without breaking. Divide into 6 pieces and roll out by hand, add the filling and sealing the edges with your fingers.

To cook in the tandır, stick the böreks on the dampened walls of the tandır, with the sealed edges touching the wall. Alternatively, place the böreks on a greased baking tray and bake them for 30 minutes in a preheated oven at 250°C. When you remove them from the oven, open the tops of the böreks, using your hands, and place slivers of butter inside. Serve hot.

Sweets

'Or have you become a fly around these sticky sweets made from honey?' D3:109-C:875

Many of the sweets from Mevlana's era are still available in present-day Konya cuisine. Helva, being Mevlana's favourite sweet, attracts particular interest. Syrupy sweets, like kadayıf, baklava, lalanga; aşure, palüze, zerde (sweet, gelatinous dessert, coloured and flavoured with saffron); and fruit and vegetable sweets made with pekmez (grape syrup) are all mentioned by Mevlana. The couplet above tells us that honey or pekmez were used as sweeteners in that era. There are other couplets that show that sugar came from Egypt. Other sources mention the theory that during that era, at big ceremonies open to the general public, special guests were served sugar sherbet while common people were given honey sherbet.

Since the thirteenth century dessert making in Konya cuisine has developed and the variety of sweets in Konya has greatly increased. The lalanga lokma mentioned by Mevlana has become kaygana, a sweet dessert made with eggs, and sweets are now prepared with sugar. The tradition of honey and pekmez continued until the 1980s. One of my sources from Konya whom I met in 1979 said, 'You can only make kadayıf with pekmez if you have money'. Today it has become expensive, and the use of honey and pekmez has declined. It is only older people used to those those flavours who prepare sweets like jams with pekmez, snow helva or honey helva.

Out of the rich selection of sweets in Konya, this section contains those mentioned by Mevlana in his works.

PASTRY SWEETS

Baklava

'What a kiss, what a kiss, neither helva nor samsa baklava are as sweet; it even draws milk gushing from stone; dig not, the spade has not the power for that.' D5:468-C:6404

Until the early years of the Republic, samsa baklava was prepared in the same way as classic baklava in Istanbul cuisine. Later it began to be prepared with flaky or filo pastry. However, other types of baklava are more common in Anatolia. Because samsa also means triangle, perhaps the baklava mentioned above refers to the type of baklava known as muska baklava.

(A muska is a written charm folded into a triangle and worn by the person who hopes to benefit from it.) Muska baklava is a variety that is folded into a triangle once the pastry has been rolled out and the filling added. In Konya muska baklav a is not prepared as frequently as other varieties. I remember eating triangular baklava only when I was a child.

The tradition of cutting baklava into triangles, as witnessed by Mevlanain his youth still exists today. Gölpınarlı also refers to the sweet as samsa baklava. My recipe is therefore for triangular baklava.

The speciality of homemade baklava in Konya is that it is soft and crisp at the same time (Doughy baklava is looked down on in Konya.). This combination is achieved by using water combined with with ashes for the pastry, and obtaining the correct consistency for the syrup. Oak ashes from trunks that have been burned in a stove or fireplace are sifted and then soaked overnight. The water that rises to the surface is collected and used for mixing the pastry. The sugar syrup should have a thick consistency. It's likely that in that era baklava, like kadayıf, was sweetened with honey or pekmez. I have therefore included honey and pekmez syrup in the recipe, as well as sugar. We do not know for certain what they used instead of lemon for their sugar syrup at that time. For this reason I have added lemon to the sugar syrup, as we do today. When making syrup with honey take care to boil the water before adding the honey. Bring to a boil, stirring continuously, and remove from the heat immediately, to make sure the honey will not turn bitter. Pekmez syrup should be prepared in the same way as honey syrup.

Serves 11 or more

For the baklava filling

— 250g or 2 cups shelled walnuts, almonds or pistachios
— 1 tbsp caster sugar

For the syrup (kestirme) Sugar syrup

— 750g or 3 ⅓ cups caster sugar
— 600ml or 2 ½ cups water
— 1 tbsp lemon juice (used nowadays, not in Mevlana's time)

Honey syrup

— 800ml or 3 ⅓ cups water
— 750g or 2 cups honey

Pekmez syrup

— 800ml or 3 ⅓ cups water
— 1kg or 2 ¼ lb pekmez

For the baklava pastry

— 375g or 3 ¾ cups strong white plain flour
— 375g or 3 ¾ cups self-raising flour
— 1 egg
— 200ml or ¾ cup water with ashes, water or milk
— 2 tbsps melted butter
— 1 tbsp wine vinegar
— 1 tsp salt
— 150g or 1 ½ cups plain flour and 150g or 1 ½ cups cornstarch, for rolling out flour
— 125g or ½ cup melted butter or clarified butter, for brushing pastry sheets
— 500g or 2 ¼ cups butter for pouring over baklava before baking

You will need a baking tray 40–45cm in diameter. Grease it with 1 tbsp of butter or clarified butter. Pound the walnuts, almonds or pistachios for the filling and mix with sugar.

Put a saucepan on to heat with the water for the syrup, the sugar and lemon juice. Stir until the sugar has dissolved. When it begins to boil turn down the heat, boil for two minutes and remove from heat. If you are making honey or pekmez syrup, boil the water, add the honey or pekmez, stirring continuously, and remove from the heat when it begins to boil.

Sift the flour on to a pastry board, break the egg into it, add the water, melted butter, vinegar and salt. Gathering the flour from the centre, knead into a soft, pliable dough. It is ready when it stretches like chewing gum instead of breaking when picked up. Once it has reached the desired consistency, divide the dough into 20 pieces. Allow to rest under a damp cloth for at least 30 minutes.

Mix the flour with the cornstarch. Roll out paper-thin sheets of pastry and place them in the baking tin. Brush the pastry with the melted butter after every two layers, piling the sheets on top of each other. When you have placed half the sheets into the baking tin in this way, add the filling, then continue to add the layers of pastry, brushing with butter after every two layers, as before. Dip the edge of a sharp knife into melted butter, press it down and cut into triangles without lifting the blade of the knife.

Drizzle the hot baklava butter over the top. Preheat the oven to 200°C and bake the baklava for 30–40 minutes. When it comes out of the oven pour the hot, but not boiling, syrup evenly over the top.

HELVA

'In the hearts of gentle mens love every sorrow is wine, roasted meat, sugar, helva.' D3:435 C:4182, M3:540-C:4534

'The soul granted it by God eats helva,
not the one whose fingers are longest.' M3:540-C:4534

Helva is the sweet mentioned most frequently in Mevlana's works. In his book, *Conversations*, ('Makalat 1') Shems-i Tebrizi spoke of pekmez helva in the following way:

By caressing gradually you get crystalised sugar from sugar cane,
With time you get satin from silkworms,
Perform your tasks slowly, with patience,
The day will come when you get helva from verjuice.
Makalat 1, p:354

Irene Melinkoff writes that helva ceremonies were held in Mevlana's time. We can therefore say that the Ottoman Sultans' helva gatherings date as far back as the Seljuks. Helva gatherings were a regular occurrence in Konya until recently. As Saadet Ongun writes, 'In the Konya of the 1950s people often went to each other's houses on cold winter evenings. Guests arriving after dinner were first served arabaşı soup (a hot chicken soup served with cold dough) or papara (a dish made with dried bread and broth), followed by peşmane, or pişmaniye, (a sweet with a texture similar to candyfloss), prepared by the men, or hemp helva prepared by the lady of the house. Other helvas were also prepared if desired.' The arrival of television has meant that helva gatherings have become increasingly rare.

As there is a couplet that is so reminiscent of snow helva, which still exists in Konya today, I saw fit to include the recipe. Mevlana mentions sugar, whereas in Konya snow helva is prepared with pekmez. Nowadays in Konya we prepare all the helvas included below, as well as semolina helva, not mentioned by Mevlana. Helva is served to welcome newborn babies into the world, as well as to bid farewell to those who have died. It is eaten at all ceremonies between birth and death, such as engagements, weddings and circumcisions.

Although helva can be made using any flour, it is truly exceptional when made with the strong plain flour known in Turkey as 'homemade flour'.

Almond Helva

'Before such a soul a beauty appears with every breath, to that soul, who alone can see it, a beauty comes with every breath, offering dishes of never before seen almond helva.' D4:430-C:4154

'The respectful shall receive respect; those who bring sugar shall eat almond helva.' M1:315-C:1500

In my recipe for almond helva I have used sugar, the luxury item of the era, as the sweetener. If you prefer, you can make this recipe by adding 200–400g of honey, according to taste, instead of sugar.

Serves 4 or more

— 250g or 1 cup butter
— 2 tbsps blanched almonds
— 100g or 1 cup strong plain flour
— 100g or 1 cup wholemeal flour
— 450g or 2 cups sugar
— 800ml or 3 ⅓ cups water
— 1 tbsp rose water

Melt the butter in a round-bottomed pan. Add the almonds to the flour and cook on a very low heat, stirring with a wooden spoon, for approximately 60 minutes, until the almonds and flour have turned golden brown. (A good helva needs to cook for at least 60 minutes.)

Put the sugar and water on to heat in a saucepan and stir until the sugar has dissolved. Remove from the heat two minutes after it has come to a boil and pour on to the cooked flour mixture in its pan and stir. Once it has stopped sticking to the pan, cover and leave on a very low heat for 15 minutes.

Spoon the helva into a dish, smoothing the surface with the back of a spoon, sprinkle with rose water and serve hot.

Honey Helva

'Hoping to acquire merit in God's eyes he presented them with hot bread and a large dish of helva made with honey.' M4: 373-C:2401

Serves 5 or more
— 250g or 1 cup butter
— 100g or 1 cup strong plain flour

- 100g or 1 cup wholemeal flour
- ½ kg or 1 ½ cups honey (or less if you prefer your helva less sweet)
- 400ml or 1 ¾ cups water

Melt the butter in a round-bottomed pan. Add the flour and cook on a very low heat for approximately 60 minutes until the flour turns golden brown. Mix the honey with the hot water (it should not be boiled, or it will turn bitter) and add to the flour mixture, stirring continuously. When it no longer sticks to the side of the pan, cover and leave on a very low heat for 15 minutes.

Spoon the helva into a dish, pressing it down with the back of a spoon to obtain a smooth surface, and serve hot.

Snow Helva

'Let us kiss his lips when it is snowing,
because snow with sugar refreshes the heart.' D:267-C:1750

This snow helva made with pekmez is eaten on winter evenings in Konya. It is bound to have been tried with sugar which was such a luxury in that era.

Serves 4

- 4 bowls of snow
- 4 tbsps grape pekmez (a little more or a little less, according to taste)

After it has snowed, wait for a few days for the frost to settle. When the snow has become light and fluffy, go to a clean area somewhere high up, discard the upper layer and scoop snow into bowls with a spoon. Drizzle the pekmez over the top and serve to your guests.

Pekmez (Black) Helva

'Before each tree he placed helva,
created with neither pekmez nor fat.' D:343-2576

This is a delicious helva that is still prepared in Konya today.

Serves 4
— 125g or ½ cup melted, clarified butter
— 100g or 1 cup wholemeal flour
— 50ml or ¼ cup milk or water
— 200g or 1 cup pekmez

Cook the flour in the melted butter on a very low heat until it turns golden brown, approximately 60 minutes. Stir the milk and pekmez together. Remove the cooked flour mixture from the heat and pour in the pekmez and milk. Return to the heat and stir until it no longer sticks to the pan. Allow to rest for 15 minutes and arrange on a dish, smoothing it out with the back of a spoon.

Helva Prepared with Sugar

'This mortal laughs when he sees God's satisfaction,
mishaps are as helva made with sugar to him.' M3:223-C:1915

'Every sugar cane comes to the temple and fastens its belt of service;
sugar too is coming to serve your helva.' D2:54-C:337

The most common helva prepared in Anatolia and Konya today is the variety made with sugar.

Serves 5 or more

- 250g or 1 cup butter
- 100g or 1 cup strong plain flour
- 100g or 1 cup wholemeal flour
- 450g or 2 cups sugar
- 800ml or 3 ⅓ cups water

Melt the butter in a round-bottomed pan. Add the flour and cook on a very low heat, stirring continuously with a wooden spoon, until it has turned golden brown. (A good helva needs to be cooked for at least 60 minutes.)

Put the sugar and water on to heat in a saucepan and stir until the sugar has dissolved. Remove from the heat 2 minutes after it has come to a boil and pour into the cooked flour mixture, stirring continuously. When it no longer sticks to the pan, cover and allow to rest for 15 minutes.

Arrange the helva on a dish and serve hot.

KADAYIF

Kadayıf and Lokm Kadayif

'Both to that faithful man and that hungry sheikh the death of their sons seems as kadayıf.' M3:223-C:1919

'Come, wine is gushing from the ewer: don't soil your bodies for mere kadayıf, or cornstarch pudding.' D3:168-C:1491

Kadayıf, which I encountered frequently in Seljuk sources, was probably prepared at home and cut by hand in that era in the following way. I believe the names tel (strand), bread, Arab and stone kadayıf weregiven to later kadayıfs.

We know that in the Konya tradition it would have been sweetened with honey and pekmez.

Sabriye Erkoç told me, when I met her in 1979, that her maternal and paternal grandmothers used to make kadayıf cut by hand at home and that it was exquisite. She said, however, that for the sake of convenience they had since started to make their desserts with shop-bought tel kadayıf cut into tiny strands.

This kadayıf is quite difficult and time-consuming to make, but it is such an indescribable pleasure to eat, and quite delicious made with any of the three syrups. Nowadays, as with baklava, we use lemon with sugar syrup. If you are going to eat the kadayıf straight away you can make it without the lemon to get a taste of the flavour of that era.

Serves 11 or more

For the filling

— 150g or 1 ⅓ cups shelled, crushed walnuts

For the kadayıf dough

— 250g or 2 heaped cups flour – half strong white plain and half self-raising
— 2 eggs
— 100ml or ½ cup water
— ½ tsp salt

For rolling out the dough

— 100g or 1 cup plain flour
— 100g or 1 cup cornstarch

For pouring over the kadayıf

— 250g or 1 cup clarified butter
— 1 piece of bread

For the syrup Sugar syrup

— 375g or 1 ⅔ cups caster sugar
— 300ml or 1 ¼ cups water
— 1 tsp lemon juice (not used in Mevlana's era)

Honey syrup

— 400ml or 1 ¾ cups water
— 375g or 1 cup honey

Pekmez syrup

— 400ml or 1 ¾ cups water
— 200g or 1 cup pekmez

Grease a baking tin, 35cm in diameter, with 1 tbsp of butter or clarified butter.

Sift the flour on to a pastry board, break the eggs into it and add the water and salt. Knead, mixing from the centre, to make a soft, pliable dough. Divide into 8 pieces. Allow to rest under a damp cloth for at least 30 minutes.

Mix the flour and cornstarch. Roll out each piece of dough to the thickness of a knife blade (3mm) and allow to rest for a few minutes on a cloth. Place two of the partially dried sheets of dough on top of one another, wrap around the rolling pin and then slowly withdraw it from under the dough. With a sharp knife cut the pastry, now in the shape of a roll, into tiny strands the thickness of tel kadayıf (like shredded wheat). Spread out the strands of dough on a cloth and allow to rest again for a few minutes without allowing them to dry out. Repeat with the other sheets.

Arrange half the kadayıf in the pan, taking care not to let it dry out too much. Sprinkle the walnuts on top. Cover with the remaining kadayıf. Cut into squares.

Heat the clarified butter in the pan with the piece of bread. When the bread turns golden remove the pan from the heat. Wait until the butter has cooled down and drizzle over the kadayıf (if you pour boiling butter over the kadayıf it may collapse). Bake in an oven preheated to 200°C for approximately 30 minutes, until the kadayıf has turned light brown. Remove and allow to cool.

Put the sugar, water and lemon juice in a saucepan to make the syrup. Stir on the heat until the sugar has dissolved. When it begins to boil lower the heat, cook for 2 minutes and remove from the heat. For honey and pekmez syrup boil the water first, add the honey or pekmez, stirring continuously. When it comes to a boil remove from heat (it will turn bitter if overboiled) and wait until it has cooled slightly. Pour the hand-hot syrup over the cold kadayıf. Wait three to four hours, until it has absorbed the syrup, and serve.

Milk Puddings and Light Sweets

Aşure

'On aşure day all the Aleppans remain at the door of Antakya till nightfall.' M6:135-C:780

Gölpınarlı mentions that dervishes referred to aşure as aş (cooked food) and that it was passed down to the Mevlevi Sufis from the Alevites.

He describes how in the month of Muharram, the first month of the Muslim calendar, aşure was prepared in tekkes in large cauldrons for the souls of those killed in Kerbala, that the dervishes took turns in stirring it in the form of a double letter vav in Arabic and that sheikhs from other tekkes were invited to a dinner at which it was served. Aşure, which is prepared in many Islamic countries and in the whole of Anatolia, is also prepared in Konya. My mother, Hanım Halıcı, talked of how the tekke in Konya used to distribute aşure to the public before it was closed down. In the Konya of today, which is now mostly blocks of flats, throughout an entire month neighbours cook this very popular dish as they drop in on each other for a chat. Moreover, political parties and large grocery stores prepare aşure during the month of Muharram and distribute it to the public. In Konya roasted hemp is also sprinkled on to aşure.

Serves 5 or more

— 35g or 1 tbsp chick peas
— 35g or 1 tbsp white haricot beans
— 150g or ¾ cup bulgur wheat
— 75g or ½ cup rice
— 2 litres or 8 ⅓ cups water
— 25g or 1 tbsp sultanas or currants
— 2 dried figs
— 3–4 dried apricots
— 300g or 1 ⅓ cup sugar or 200g or 1 cup pekmez, or more to taste
— 50g or ½ cup walnuts
— 50g or ⅓ cup hazelnuts
— 50g or ½ cup pistachio nuts
— 50g or ½ cup hemp seeds, toasted in a dry frying pan

Soak the chick peas and beans in water overnight. The following morning change the water and boil for approximately one hour, until they are soft. Put the bulgur and rice on to heat with the water. When the mixture becomes soft add the chick peas, beans, chopped figs, apricots and sultanas or currants and boil for 30 minutes until it has become thick and soupy. Add the pekmez or sugar and boil for another 15–20 minutes, stirring occasionally to prevent it from sticking to the bottom of the pan. When it cools, ladle into dishes and decorate with roasted walnuts, hazelnuts, pistachio nuts and hemp seeds.

Water Pudding

Palüze (Pelte)

'You have such flavour, so sweet are you that buttered, honeyed delicacies are as nothing to you; roast in your own fat, become sweet with your own honey, besides, you are paluze, pure taste.' D4:C.124:1105

'Pretend you have not tasted this paluze, or seen this kitchen before you.' M5:C.315-1965

In Konya, palüze is taken to women who have just given birth to improve their milk supply, but nowadays it is prepared with sugar instead of honey.

Serves 5 or more

— 800ml or 3 ⅓ cups water
— 75g or ¾ cups wheatstarch
— 100ml or ½ cup water (for mixing the wheatstarch)
— 225g or 1 ½ cups honey
— ½ tsp cinnamon or 1 tsp rose water

Put the water on to heat. When it begins to boil mix the wheatstarch with the 100ml water and pour it slowly into the boiling water, stirring continuously. After 10 minutes, when it has thickened, add the honey, stirring all the time. When it comes to a boil remove from the heat and transfer to a bowl. After it has cooled sprinkle with cinnamon or rose water and serve.

Walnuts with Pekmez

This delicious dish, also served at Mevlana's table, adds a special touch to breakfast.

Serves 5

— 100g or 1 cup shelled walnuts
— 200g or 1 cup pekmez
— 50ml or ¼ cup water

Cut the walnuts in 8 pieces and put them in a saucepan. Add the pekmez and water. Heat on a medium flame. When it comes to a boil turn the heat down to low and simmer for 5 minutes. Spoon into bowls and serve.

Rice Pudding with Saffron

Zerde with Saffron

'O saffron, drink water until you become saffron,
and only then enter the zerde.' M4:157-C:1080

'There are some people who cannot eat honey on its own but can only eat it by mixing it with zerde, rice, helva or other food.' FM:300

Nowadays zerde is also made with sugar instead of honey. Zerde made with honey has a very special flavour. The elderly ladies in Konya have informed me that in the past it was also made with pekmez.

Serves 4

— ¼ tsp saffron
— 1 tbsp water (for soaking the saffron)
— 75g or ⅓ cup long grain rice
— 1 litre or 1 ¾ pints water
— 150g or ⅔ cup sugar or 225g or ⅔ cup strained honey
— 1 tbsp rose water

Soak the saffron in the tablespoon of water overnight. The following morning pick over the rice and wash. Cover with warm water and leave to soak until the water has cooled. Put the rice and water on to heat in a saucepan. When it boils turn the heat down to very low and simmer for approximately 30 minutes until the rice is completely soft. When it has reached the desired consistency, add half the sugar, then stir in the other half when it starts to boil. After 10–15 minutes, when the rice has thickened, strain the saffron and add the water to the rice. When it starts to boil pour into dishes. If you are using honey add it, stirring continuously, when the saffron comes to a boil. Bring to the boil again and pour into dishes. Sprinkle with rose water when it cools.

Apricot Compote

Apricot Hoşaf

'A man was shaking an apricot tree and helping himself to the fruit. The owner of the property asked him Have you no fear of God? The man said Why should I? The tree is God's tree and I am one of God's mortals, God's mortal is eating God's property.

'Thinking, I'll show him, the owner of the orchard brought a rope, tied the man to the tree and began to beat him with a stick. When the man said Have you no fear of God? the owner of the orchard said Why should I? You're God's mortal and this is God's stick, I'm beating God's mortal with God's stick.' FM:233

'It is likely that in those days apricots were made into sherbet, as well as eaten fresh. Eflaki mentions apricot hoşaf.'
The Book of the Wise 2, p:220

As in many other parts of Anatolia, hoşaf is served at traditional meals in Konya and is known as 'the silencer'. When hoşaf appears on the table it is understood that there will be no other dishes to follow and the guests fill themselves up with the last dish to have been served.

Serves 4

- 150g or 1 cup dried apricots
- 1 litre or 1 ¾ pints water
- Grape syrup (pekmez) to taste, or 200g or 1 cup sugar

Wash the apricots and put them on to heat in a saucepan with the water. After 5 minutes, when the water comes to a boil, turn the heat down to low and simmer for 10 minutes. Add the sugar and cook for another 10 minutes. When it cools, transfer to a large bowl and serve.

Bread and Dishes Prepared with Bread

'Without fire in the heart's tandır or the stomach's oven,
He cooks bread and puts it out for sale, but our baker is invisible, indiscernible to the eye.' D2:364-C:3036

'How can my tree be cheerful while spring does not touch its visage, if you do not knead my dough, how will my yeast make it rise?'
D1:286-C:2659

'A loaf on the table is lifeless,
but inside a body it becomes an animated spirit.' M1:313-C:1480

'It can never come to life in the table's centre; but the soul kneads it with water of life, transforms it into life.' M1:313-C:1481

'He who listens is like the water before a chef kneading dough. Words too resemble water. It is added to flour in the right measure.' FM:49

'How can anyone's dough remain raw if kneaded by God?
I am dough that admits yeast, no yeastless bulamaç5 dough am I.'
D3:265-C:2544

'With your fire, my face glowed bright red, like a loaf baked in your heat; but now I have crumbled to dust like stale bread, and been scattered on the ground; come, gather me up from the dirt on the roads.' D3:269-C:2575

Mevlana mentions loaves of bread, yufka, bazlama, tandır, corn and barley bread. With the exceptions of corn and barley bread, all these breads are still prepared in Konya today.

Bread is the staple food of Turks, therefore any meal is *katık*: an accompaniment for bread. For this reason, a lot of care is taken over the quality of bread in Anatolia, and it is consequently delicious, so much so that during the years of the Second World War the bread in Konya became katık for bread. Old people relate how loaves of bread baked in commercial bakeries and bought with ration cards were wrapped up as the filling inside homemade yufka bread and eaten.

Flat Bread

Bazlama

'How can the peasant conceive of the Sultan's treasures; the lowly Kurd desires only bazlama and ayran.' D:282-C:1911

Bazlama can be either eaten as bread or spread with butter when it comes out of the saç, in which case it is called 'gözleme'. It is folded over in a half moon shape with various fillings and also eaten as börek.

For 2 bazlamas

For the raising agent

- 1 tbsp yogurt
- 1 tbsp warm water
- 2 tbsps plain flour

For the bread

- 100g or 1 cup plain flour
- 100g or 1 cup strong plain flour
- 100g or 1 cup wholemeal flour
- 2 tbsps raising agent
- 2 tbsps water
- 200ml or 1 cup warm water
- ¼ tsp salt

Mix the yogurt, water and flour in a bowl the night before you wish to bake. Cover, wrap with a cloth and leave in a warm place overnight.

Sift all the flour, make a well in the centre and add the 2 tbsps of raising agent and the 2 tbsps water and mix well. Take a little flour and mix to the consistency of thick set yogurt, pile the flour on the top and sprinkle the salt around the edges. When cracks begin to appear on the surface of the flour knead with 200ml warm water until you have a fairly stiff dough. Cover and leave to stand in a warm place for at least two hours. Divide into 3 pieces and roll out in 1cm thick circles the size of a pasta bowl. Place inside a saç or wok on a very low heat, cook for 5–6 minutes. Turn over when the first side is done and cook the other side.

Tandır Bread

'The world is a tandır, where there are loaves of every shade; but no one who has set eyes on the baker has any use for the tandır, or need for bread.' D3:219-:C:2048

Tandır bread is a Konya bread still baked in houses that have tandırs. It is delicious when made with strong plain flour. No other bread smells quite like tandır bread fresh from the oven.

For 3 loaves

— Temperature of tandır: The flames should have died down, and the embers should be glowing.
— 100g or 1 cup plain flour
— 100g or 1 cup strong plain flour
— 100g or 1 cup wholemeal flour
— 2 tbsps raising agent (see Bazlama, p. 137)
— 1 tbsp warm water
— ½ tsp salt
— 300ml or 1 ¼ cups warm water

Sift all the flour on to a pastry board. Make a well in the centre, add the raising agent and 1 tbsp water and mix well. Take in a little flour, pile the remaining flour on top and sprinkle with salt. When cracks begin to appear in the flour, make another well in the centre, mix with the warm water to make a fairly stiff dough. Leave to rise under a damp cloth until it is stringy and elastic when stretched, about 30 minutes. Divide the dough into three pieces, using your hands, shape into loaves, wet the walls of the tandır with water and attach the loaves to them.

Bake. If you are going to bake the bread in the oven, form the dough into oval shapes and slap it with the back of your hand to flatten it. Place the loaves on a greased baking sheet and bake in a preheated oven at 250°C for 30 minutes.

Bread Soaked in Meat and Meat Juices

Meat Tirit

'Stop this talk now; cover the tandır; cover it so they can turn the bread inside into tirit.' D5:125-C:1438

'Since seeing your table, your nutriment, I no longer endure tirit; I have seen your existence and evaded my own ever since.' D1:287-C:2660

Tirit is very common in Konya nowadays and is also prepared using all kinds of vegetables. My recipe, however, is for the tirit served at traditional meals. This tirit occupies a special place on the menu of Konya wedding banquets and is served to thousands of guests. The preparation of the wedding feast begins one day in advance. The meat is the first thing that is prepared. In the evening close relatives are invited to eat 'tirit'. The chef prepares the following tirit for the guests on the groom's side. He also sends some to the bride's house, for the bride's mother. In return, the bride's mother sends the head chef and all the other chefs either a tip or a gift. Nowadays we use parsley instead of mint.

Serves 4

— ½ kg or 1lb 2oz bony mutton

— 1 litre or 4 cups water
— Salt to taste
— 3 loaves of tandır bread cut up into chunks
— 4 onions, thinly sliced
— 1 tsp salt
— 1 tsp sumach
— 1 bunch fresh mint, chopped

Wash the meat and put it on to heat. When it comes to the boil skim off the foam that forms on top with a perforated ladle. Cover and cook for approximately 60–70 minutes, until the meat comes away from the bone. Add the salt and remove from the heat after 5 minutes. Place the bread in a large dish. Mix the onions with the salt and set aside for 5 minutes. Rub by hand, wash, squeeze well and arrange on top of the bread. Sprinkle with sumach. Debone the slightly cooled meat, shred it and scatter over the bread in the dish, sprinkle the chopped mint around the edges and serve.

Wafer-Thin Griddled Bread

Yufka Bread (Saç Bread)

'I am in this world, but my heart did not order me to succumb to greed and, by flattening, pulling and stretching, make a half yufka round.'

DI:321-C:2968

Yufka bread is approximately 50–60cm in diameter and paper-thin.Traditionally all the neighbours get together and cook large quantities in a saç, which can then be kept in a cool place for two or three months. Just before it is eaten it is wetted on a tablecloth to soften it, folded into four and placed inside a saucepan to prevent it from drying out again. It is served as an accompaniment. It is also served rolled up with various fillings as a 'dürüm' (roll).

To make 6

— 100g or 1 cup plain flour
— 100g or 1 cup strong plain flour
— 100g or 1 cup wholemeal flour
— 300ml or 2 ½ cups water
— ½ tsp salt

Sift the flour, add the salt and water and knead to make a dough. Divide into 6 pieces and allow to rest for about 30 minutes under a damp cloth on a wooden board sprinkled with flour. Roll out very thinly with a rolling pin to a diameter of 50–60cm. Cook both sides in a saç or wok on a low heat for 3–4 minutes, turning occasionally.

Milk Bread

Cörek

'Watching them bake camel- and lion-shaped çörek whets the children's appetites, and they sink their teeth into their hands.'
M6:705-C:4729

'If the taste I have in my mouth today, as though I were eating buttered, honeyed çörek, is not the taste and flavour of those beautiful, immeasurably sweet lips, then I don't know what it is.' D3:259-C:2464

Çörek is generally a savoury bread eaten between meals. The sweet variety is known as kurabiye. Savoury çörek is also eaten at breakfast, dipped into pekmez or honey.

In the olden days in Konya, çörek or kurabiye prepared at home and baked at local bakeries was served at the ceremonial *hamam* of a prospective bride.

I have not been able to work out whether the çörek made in the shape of camels and lions was shaped by hand or with a cutter. In present day-Konya çörek is the size of a hand and oval-shaped, while kurabiye can be oval or round.

To make 15 Çöreks

— 200ml or 1 cup milk
— 125g or ½ cup sheep's-tail fat or clarified butter
— 1 egg
— 1 tbsp raising agent or 1 tsp dried yeast
— 1 tsp salt
— 300g or 2 ½ generous cups strong plain flour

For the top

— 1 tbsp plain yogurt
— 1 tbsp clarified butter or sheep's-tail fat
— 1 tbsp black cumin seed

In a bowl mix all the ingredients for the çörek and knead into a dough. Cover and leave in a warm place for 30 minutes (depending on the temperature it may require more or less time to rise). Break off pieces of the risen dough and shape into long çöreks the size of a hand. Place in a greased baking tin. Allow to stand for another 10–20 minutes, carve square shapes on them with the back of a knife. Beat the yogurt and butter together and brush the çörek with it. Sprinkle with the black cumin seeds and bake in a tandır or in a preheated oven at 200°C for 20–25 minutes.

Drinks

'Hundreds of fruits, like sherbet bottles; each with its own special taste.' d5:350-c:4403

'Since you told me you were ill thousands of health restoring sherbets have boiled ecstatically, with love and protection.' d3:262-c:2503

Konya cuisine boasts a large variety of drinks and sherbets right from the thirteenth century to the present day. Honey sherbet, milk and honey sherbet, rose water sherbet, fig sherbet, pomegranate sherbet, sugar sherbet, milk and sugar sherbet and grape şıra (slightly fermented grape must) are Mevlana's sherbets. Apart from fig sherbet, all these sherbets are still drunk in Konya today. There is no mention, in any of the books, of verjuice and pekmez sherbet that form part of Konya cuisine. Wine, ayran (yogurt with water and salt) and coffee are also popular. We know from Mevlana's works that coffee, which did not arrive in Istanbul until the sixteenth century, was already being drunk in Konya in the thirteenth century.

Today, in addition to homemade sherbets, factory-produced fruit juices, fizzy and cola drinks are also very popular.

Yogurt with Water and Salt

Ayran

'Just as the fat in ayran is hidden,
the essence of truth is buried in lies.' M4:425-C:3030

' You have fallen into his ayran, no matter, for you were born
of his love. Run a thousand leagues if you wish,
there's no escaping this idol.' D1:164-C:1550

Ayran is the Turkish national drink. It is also the principal drink in Mevlevi cuisine, and is drunk widely throughout Anatolia as well as in Konya.

Serves 4

— 250g or 1 cup strained thick set yogurt
— 800ml or 3 ⅓ cups water
— Salt to taste

Place the yogurt in a bowl. Add the water gradually, beating all the time with a spoon or whisk. Add the salt, pour into a decanter and serve.

Honey Sherbet

'Hush, silence is even better than drinking honey sherbet.
Burn words, renounce hints and insinuations.' D2:5-C:25

Honey sherbet is drunk very rarely these days.

Serves 4

— 1.2 litres or 5 cups warm water
— 4 tsp honey (or more, depending on taste) with honeycomb, strained without using heat

Mix the honey with the warm water. Strain through a clean cheesecloth. Chill in a cool place, pour into glasses and serve.

Milk and Honey Sherbet

'O indomitable sun, O insubordinate beauty,
you have been reconciled with the milky way in the heavens;
like milk and honey you have fused with mortals, become one.'
D1:181-C:1727

'Once more they have combined milk with honey,
they have joined the lovers together again.' D4:165-C:1512

'It is the rays of the heart shining on to them that illuminate the beauty of milk and honey, the heart shows the beauty of every beautiful thing.' M3:252-C:2266

Milk and honey sherbet is still drunk today.

Serves 4

— 800ml or 3 ⅓ cups warm milk
— 4 tsps honey with honeycomb strained without using heat

Stir the milk and honey until all the honey has dissolved. Strain through a clean cheesecloth. Chill in a cool place, pour into glasses and serve.

Rosewater Sherbet

'The confusing words he uttered cast poison into the sugared rose water sherbet.' M1:139-C:450

'He stooped and bowed and scraped to him, and served him unadulterated, pure rose water sherbet.' M3:68-C:568

In present times rose water sherbet is prepared only on special occasions.

Serves 4

— 50g or 2 tbsps fragrant, pink, ever-blooming rose petals
— 150g or ⅔ cup caster sugar
— 1 litre or 4 cups water

Remove the white edges of the rose petals with a pair of scissors. In a bowl rub them with half of the sugar and set aside for an hour. Boil the water with the rest of the sugar, then remove from the heat. When it has cooled down a little add the rose petals. Strain through gauze when cooled completely. Pour into glasses and serve. This sherbet will be even more delicious if it is prepared the night before and strained the following morning.

Fig Sherbet

'Every pleasure experienced without you is unripe fig syrup, a snake bite.' D5: 328-C:4015

From the 1950s to the present day I have never once encountered or heard of fig sherbet in Konya. Figs are used in sweets and in aşure. The following experiment turned into a sherbet, which I would recommend to anyone looking for an original flavour.

Serves 4

— 4 dried figs
— 800ml or 3 ⅓ cups water
— 50ml grape pekmez or 4 tsps sugar (a little more or less, according to taste)

Boil the figs for approximately 30–40 minutes, until they disintegrate. Remove from heat. Empty into a strainer set over a bowl. Push the figs through (alternatively you may use a hand whisk). Strain through a fine sieve. If some of the water has evaporated, add more to make up 4 glasses and return to heat. Bring to the boil and remove from the heat. Add the pekmez or sugar and bring to the boil again. Cool, pour into sherbet glasses and serve.

Pomegranate Sherbet

'The sweet ones become pomegranate sherbet; but of the rotten ones only the voice remains.' m1:162-c:713

Pomegranate sherbet is rarely prepared today. It is more common to drink freshly squeezed pomegranate juice.

Serves 4

— 200ml or 1 cup freshly squeezed pomegranate juice
— 150g or ⅔ cup caster sugar
— 800ml or 3 ⅓ cups water

Stir the pomegranate juice, sugar and water in a bowl until the sugar has dissolved. Strain through gauze. Chill in a cool place. When cold pour into glasses and serve.

To make pomegranate juice roll an uncut fresh pomegranate underfoot on the floor, make an incision and squeeze it over a juicer.

Sugar Sherbet

'How can this nine-year-old vinegar suffice for someone in the land of sugar drinking glass after glass of sugar sherbet?' D:106-C:161

'Kemaleddin Kabi related the following legend: When I realised the extent of Mevlana's greatness I consulted my beloved friends and said I insist on performing the sema for Hazreti Mevlana and becoming his disciple. They searched Konya high and low but could not find more than thirty bags of pure crystalised sugar. I went to Gömeç Hatun, the Sultan's wife, who gave me ten more bags. Convinced this quantity of sugar would not be enough for everyone, I thought we could make honey sherbet for the ordinary people. At that point Mevlana arrived and ordered Kemaleddin; if there are a lot of guests

and there isn't enough sherbet, add more water. In response to this, I threw all the sugar into the pool of the Karatay madrasah, made several large ewers of sherbet and sent them to the Sultan's taster to taste. He filled a bowl and gave it to me. It was very sweet, therefore they added water. I tasted it again, it was even sweeter. They filled ten more ewers of sherbet from the pool, again it was sweet. In response I cried out that it was Mevlana who had performed this great miracle. That night I invited all the Sultans and exalted personages. Mevlana remained in the sema from afternoon namaz until midnight. I fastened my belt of service and served sherbet in the area where shoes are removed, to everyone in the sema who was thirsty.'

Eflaki, The Book of the Wise 1, *p:179*

As can be seen, because sugar was a rare commodity in that era, sugar sherbet was a luxury. Honey sherbet was considered to be for the masses.

As in the whole of Anatolia, sugar sherbet is an absolute must at weddings and engagements in Konya.

Serves 4

— 800ml or 3 ⅓ cups warm water
— 4 tsp caster sugar (more, if desired)

Mix the sugar with the water and strain through gauze. Set aside in a cool place. When it is chilled pour into glasses and serve.

Milk Sherbet with Sugar

This drink is still very popular in present-day Konya, just as it was in Mevlana's time. It is drunk throughout Anatolia, because it is believed that the Prophet Muhammad was offered milk after the Miraç (his ascent to heaven on the back of a winged horse). Ayşe Cıvıl writes, 'Before the tariqats were closed down milk nights were celebrated at the Miraç Kandil (the annual celebration commemorating the miraç) at Mevlana's Tomb.The Whirling Prayer Ceremony (Sema) was performed and afterwards milk was served. Everyone drank their milk, recited their Fatiha and went home. I was present at the final milk night. Atatürk and Latife Hanım were there too. They watched the ceremony, the milk was handed out, they also drank and then left. The night of the Miraç is also known as milk night.'

Serves 4

— 800ml or 3 ⅓ cups milk

— 4 tsps caster sugar

Boil the milk. When it has cooled slightly, mix in the sugar. Set aside in a cool place. When it is chilled pour into glasses and serve.

Grape Must

'As grapes they are brothers; but once you squeeze and crush them they become one must.' M2:502-C:3725

This popular drink is often prepared at home when grapes are in season.

Serves 4–6

— 1 kg Konya dimnit grapes (very juicy, black, small seeded grapes, grown in Konya)

Wash the grapes and remove them from their stalks. Place the grapes in a sieve and place a bowl underneath. Using your hand squeeze the juice into the sieve, allowing it to drip into the bowl underneath. Strain through a fine meshed metal sieve. Pour into glasses and serve.

Coffee

'Our country is a land of plenty, our coffee descends from the ninth heaven, almond helva rained down on the assembly.' D2:77-C:631

'Oh my lady, fill my cup with coffee, fill it over and over again. Unhappy is he who visits you sober; he should avoid it, as should you.' D2:167-C:1338

'Though my consort, my companion, deny my devotion, still they are merciful; because I am devoted to coffee, I must drink coffee, and as for repentance, it does me no honour.' D2:274-C:2228

'A worried, anxious person is a wretched person, he perishes away with grief; let him drink our Effendi's coffee, let it intoxicate him, free him of his troubles.' D:24-C:214

Mevlana mentions coffee with almond helva, whereas in Konya it was traditionally served with lokum (Turkish delight) and water. Today coffee is also accompanied by chocolate and various sweets.

When making coffee you need to take certain precautions to ensure that you do not lose the foam at the top. You need to use the right size *cezve* (a metal pot with a handle used for preparing Turkish coffee) for the number of cups you are going to prepare. If you use a cezve for three to make two cups of coffee the coffee will not be frothy. Excessive stirring loses the foam. Moreover, when the coffee rises, if you hold the lip or spout of the cezve away from the flame and tip it up so the back of the cezve is in the centre of the flame, you will ensure that the coffee rises up towards the spout. My recipe is for orta (medium) coffee. Sade (pronounced sah-de) coffee contains no sugar, and sweet coffee contains 2 teaspoons. For the best taste, a good cup of coffee should be cooked over a low flame for at least 8 minutes.

For one person

— 1 Turkish coffee cup of water
— ½ tsp caster sugar
— 2 tsps Turkish coffee

Put the water in the cezve, add the sugar and put on to heat. When it is warm add the coffee and stir until it is completely mixed into the water. The first time it rises, spoon the froth from the top into the coffee cup. Allow the remaining coffee to come to a boil several more times, then pour on top of the froth in the cup.

Dishes Bought or Cooked Locally

'To start their day all the helva makers opened shops overflowing with sweets and nuts.' D5:53-C:634

'Just as in shops that sell cooked heads, there were countless heads, hearts in front of him; amongst those heads I found a head.' D4:25-C:186

'In the depths of winter, when hearty young boys shiver in heavy fur, even when standing beside ovens and tandırs, Hazreti Mevlana would climb up to the roof of the madrasah and, with thousands of groans and sighs, perform the ishaa namaz[6] until just before dawn.' Eflaki, *The Book of the Wise 1*, p:188

We know that it was common to buy readymade food in Mevlana's time. Helva makers, bakers and shops selling kebab and roasted sheep's head are all mentioned in his works. We also know that ovens and tandırs were used to prepare these dishes, as well as stoves.

Sheep's-Head Kebab

Kelle Kebab

'One of the disciples fancied roasted lamb's head.' FM:63

We know that in Mevlana's time roasted sheep's head, sheep's-head broth and sheep's-head tirit were considered great delicacies.

Until recent years in Konya, kelle kebab was travellers' food. At stations there was always a roasted sheep's-head vendor and people would not board the train until they had bought their kelle. Today there is only one roasted kelle vendor left in Konya. But at home kelle, sheep's trotters and, in particular, bulgur pilav made with sheep's head broth and served topped with sheep's-head, is a real treat.

Serves 1

— 1 cleaned goat's or sheep's head
— 2 litres or 8 cups water
— Salt to taste
— Bulgur pilav (cooked with sheep's-head broth)
— Fresh mint and cress

Wash the cleaned head thoroughly in several changes of water, place in a saucepan with 2 litres of water. When the water begins to boil, skim off the foam that forms on the top. Cook for approximately two–three hours (one hour in a pressure cooker) until the meat comes away from the bones. Add salt and boil for 10 more minutes.

Prepare bulgur pilav (see p. 104) with the broth from the sheep's or goat's head. If you are going to serve the head whole, brown it in the oven and place it on top of the bulgur pilav. If you prefer the homemade style, remove the meat from the bones, arrange it on top of the pilav and serve.

Flat Bread with Ground Meat

Etli Ekmek/Etli Pide

'Bread and meat are soil; eat of them sparingly, to avoid being grounded on earth, like soil.' MI:483-C:2884

This couplet seems to be pointing at Konya's famous etli ekmek. In that era, it is likely that they made etli ekmek with meat chopped using the bıçak arası technique. Etli ekmek, made with bıçak arası meat, still prepared today, shows that this dish dates back to a time preceding mincing machines.

The best etli ekmek in Anatolia is found in Konya. Nowadays we add one large chopped tomato, a few of the Konya green chillies known as 'kıl biber' and a tablespoon of parsley, to the recipe below. People also prepare the topping for etli ekmek at home and send it to etli ekmek bakeries to be cooked. I am giving the recipe using the ingredients from Mevlana's time, but I also advise you to make etli ekmek with the vegetables available today. Etli ekmek is between 80–100cm long and 12–20cm wide, depending on the dough. If cooked in a bakery oven you can make 4. To bake at home, make 8 smaller breads. If necessary, bake them in batches.

Serves 3

For the topping

— 400g or 1 ½ generous cups fatty minced lamb or lamb chopped using the bıçak arası technique, with two knives
— 1 large onion
— Sheep's-tail fat or suet (if the meat is too lean)
— Salt and black pepper to taste

For the dough

- 500g or 5 cups flour, half strong plain, half wholemeal
- 2 tbsps raising agent (see p. 138), nowadays 1 tbsp fresh yeast
- 400ml or 1 ¾ cups warm water
- 1 tsp salt

For rolling out the dough

- 150g or 1 ½ cups pure bran

For greasing the baking sheet

- 1 tbsp clarified butter

Finely chop the onion and mix it into the minced meat or meat chopped in the bıçak arası fashion. Finely chop the sheep's-tail fat and add, together with the salt and black pepper. Mix well.

Sift the flour, make a well in the centre and sprinkle the salt around the edges. Pour the raising agent into the well, add water and knead into a dough. Leave in a warm place to rise.

Divide the dough into 8 pieces. Sprinkle your board with pure bran and roll out the dough with a rolling pin. Divide the topping into eight portions and sprinkle on to the dough using your hand. Place on a greased baking sheet. Cook in a preheated oven for 7–10 minutes at 250°C. Serve with ayran (see p. 145) and chopped radishes.

Fırın Kebab (Roasted Mutton)

We can safely assume that Konya's famous roasted mutton dates back to the times of the Seljuks. Mevlana's works talk of kebab and the shops that prepare kelle kebab, roasted sheep's head. It is likely that kelle kebab and roasted mutton were prepared in the same place. However, at that time roasted sheep's head was considered to be more of a delicacy. My dear friend Kevin Guld says of roasted mutton, 'It tastes divine if you eat it with your fingers.'

You can prepare roasted mutton the easy way, by boiling it until the meat is tender and then putting it into the oven, but it will not taste as good as it will if you follow the recipe below. Moreover, if you are using lamb, it needs to go into the oven without any water as it will release enough of its own juices.

Serves 5 or more

— 1 sheep's ribcage and shank
— 400ml or 1 ¾ cups water
— 1 tsp salt

Put the salt and water into a copper roasting tin. Wash the meat and place it into the tin. Put into the oven on a very low heat. Depending on the oven temperature, cook for 4–5 hours, turning occasionally with wooden skewers (sticking metal skewers into meat impairs its flavour as it releases its juices) until it is brown and tender.

Cheese Börek

Cheese Pide

It is likely that the cheese börek, known as cheese pide, was made in the same bakeries where etli ekmek, flat bread topped with meat, was baked. By talking of 'never before seen' börek, Mevlana stressed how much variety there was. In Konya it is traditional to eat cheese börek, also known as 'shop bought börek' on Sundays. To quote the ladies in Konya: 'In Konya cheese pide is eaten for lunch on Sundays; the men take them to the bakery to be cooked and bring them back. This is the way the man of the house thanks his wife for all the delicious dishes she has prepared for him during the week. The woman who has worked hard all week becomes a queen on Sundays; but it only lasts for one day. On Mondays she goes back into the kitchen, to her stove.'

This recipe makes 8 pides if they are prepared at home, 4 if they are sent to the bakery.

Serves 4

— 2 portions cheese börek filling (see p. 110) and 1 egg and 50ml or ¼ cup water (Konya's blue cheese is perfect)
— 1 portion etli ekmek dough (see p. 157)
— 150g or 1 ½ cups bran
— 125g or ½ cup butter

Prepare the 2 portions of blue cheese börek filling and one porton of etli ekmek dough. Roll the dough out lengthwise with a rolling pin, sprinkling the board with bran. Place the filling in the centre of the dough in a rectangle 5cm wide. Fold the edges of the dough over, leaving the rectangle of cheese uncovered. Place on a greased baking tray. Cook for 7–10 minutes at 250°C. Top with small chunks of butter and serve.

Preserved Foods

'How can anyone immersed in your salt like pastırma still have flesh and skin on their body?' D4:405-C:3916

'If he befriends the vinegar ewer his wine will taste sour, the wine ewer's consorts and companions are plants destined for the pickling jar.' D3:205-C:1886

'Those not in love are only fit to be pickled; sugar is worthy of helva, the caper of vinegar.' D4:352-C:3400

Mevlana talked of preserved foods such as tarhana, pastırma, kavurma, gülbeşeker (see p. 45), pekmez, vinegar, pickles, cheese and sun-dried fruit, vegetables and meat. I have included two dishes in this section.

Fried Meat Preserved in Fat Kavurma

'Unhappy, sluggish is he who hopes it [the world] will bring him good fortune; for all his airs of greatness and grandeur he will burn and scorch like kavurma.' D2:182-C:1480

In the times before there were refrigerators, kavurma was one of the main foods prepared using preservation techniques Despite refrigeration becoming widespread, Kavurma is still popular and widely prepared today. In particular, those who slaughter animals at the Feast of the Sacrifice (Kurban Bayramı) save part of the meat for kavurma. In the Konya of days gone by people prepared different varieties of kavurma, with bony meat, chunks of meat and minced meat. There were also varieties of kavurma made with liver and, for example, cartilage, left over after the tail fat had been removed for börek filling, eaten at the light meal before bed, known in Konya as 'go to bed and drop dead.' According to Havva Beton Hanım, whom I met in 1979, the meal got its name in the following way: 'Men in the habit of staying out drinking all night would come home in the early hours and ask their wives to make them some soup or breakfast. Respect for her husband would prevent the furious wife from saying anything out loud, but to herself she would mutter, 'Eat this and then go to bed and drop dead, so you won't bother me with any more orders.' Winter dishes prepared with kavurma had an extra special flavour. When there was no food prepared, people would immediately reach into the earthenware pot for some kavurma and rustle up a very decent meal with an accompanying salad or some pickles.

— 250g or 1 cup sheep's-tail fat
— ½ kg or 1lb 2oz lamb 1 tsp salt

Wash the tail and chop finely. Wash the meat and cut into small chunks. Put the sheep's-tail fat into the saucepan first, on a medium heat. Once it begins to release its fat add the meat. Cook without covering, stirring occasionally. When the meat has reabsorbed the juices it has released, add the salt and continue to cook, stirring occasionally, until it is thoroughly browned. Remove from the heat. When it has cooled slightly place in an earthenware pot, pressing down tightly. The fat should cover it completely. If it does not, fry some more sheep's-tail fat and pour over the meat until it is completely covered. Store in a cool place.

Please note that when you are frying the meat you should remove it from the heat before all the juices have been completely absorbed, otherwise it will not last for very long. This recipe will yield about 500g kavurma.

Clusters of Bulgur Wheat with Yogurt

Tarhana

It is likely that in Mevlana's time tarhana was made as follows, as it is still made this way in many parts of Anatolia. The recipe below makes 250g or 9oz tarhana.

— 150g or 1 ½ cups ground, dehusked wheat
— 800ml or 3 ⅓ cups water
— ½ kg or 2 cups yogurt
— 1 tbsp strong plain flour

Wash the wheat and soak in water overnight. In the morning place in a saucepan with the water and boil until it disintegrates. Leave it to absorb the water, cool. Knead the yogurt, boiled wheat and flour. Form clusters in the shape of köftes, pressing the centre with your finger. Spread the clusters out on a clean cloth or wooden board. Dry in the shade over a period of 4–5 days, turning occasionally. Store in a cloth bag.

RECIPES FROM 'THE TALES OF THE WISE' AND OTHER SOURCES

This section contains a selection of dishes from the era, taken from Shams al-Din al-Eflaki's *The Tales of the Wise*, a Persian biography of the first Mevlevi masters.

Pilav with Meat

Etli Pilav

'Bahaedin-i Bahri told the following anecdote: "While I was emir I would often engage in sohbet [spiritual discussion] with hazreti Çelebi Hüsameddin. I had not yet met Hazreti Mevlana. One day Çelebi Hüsameddin honoured my household with a visit. At that moment I also saw hazreti Mevlana coming up the stairs. Mevlana said, "Emir Bahaeddin, do you mean to steal Hazreti Çelebi away from us?" When Mevlana sat down I thought about offering him some food. Just at that moment Mevlana requested, "Bring a little something to eat." I asked the servant in Greek, "What do you have prepared?" The servant replied, "We've just eaten, I've left the cauldron to soak in hot

water." Mevlana said, "Tell him to bring the cauldron." Then he asked for a pan and a bowl and dipped the bowl into the cauldron with his own hand. I saw that what came out was pilav with fried meat. It was unparalleled in exquisiteness and flavour. *We were all amazed at how so much food could have come out of an empty cauldron. Mevlana ordered, "This is celestial food, sent to us from God. It needs to be eaten."'*

Eflaki, *The Tales of the Wise 1*, p:264

Although Mevlana does mention rice in his works, I could not find the word pilav, otherwise known as 'dane' (pronounced dah-ne) in Seljuk sources. But Eflaki's pilav with fried meat lives on as Konya wedding pilav, served at functions and special occasions. This pilav, topped with fried meat, is the speciality of Konya's chefs. At weddings the team of chefs distributes the food to every table in turn. Guests are served as much rice, without meat, as they wish. Tables with special guests, however, get extra helpings of meat as well. In this case, in order to be discreet, the waiters serving the tables tell the chef 'One submarine' or 'One buried treasure' and the chef ladles the meat into the dish, covers it with rice and sends the second helping of meat to the special guests without letting the other guests see.

Serves 5 or more

— 1 lamb shank or rib cage (whole)
— 300g or 1 cup chick peas (soaked overnight)
— 1 tbsp currants soaked in water for 30 minutes
— 2 litres or 8 cups water
— 1 tsp salt
— 1 litre or 4 cups milk, boiled and cooled

— 2 servings rice pilav (see p. 105)
— 250g or 1 cup melted sheep's-tail fat or clarified butter

Wash the meat and place in a large saucepan. Add the chick peas, water and salt and put on to heat. Cook until it is tender, skimming off the foam from the top from time to time. Strain into a bowl.

Use the meat broth for the pilav and add the chick peas and currants while it is cooking. While the pilav is steeping, place the meat in the milk for 10 minutes. Heat the fat, remove the meat from the milk and brown in the fat. Arrange the pilav in a dish, place the meat on top, sprinkle with black pepper and serve.

Balkh-Özbek Pilav

Hassaten Lokma

'The Mevlevis called all food "lokma" but there was also a pilav known as "Hassaten Lokma." This pilav was Balkh-Özbek pilav, cooked with chick peas, onions, carrots, chestnuts and fatty meat. It is probably a tradition left over from Mevlana's time.'
Gölpınarlı, *The Mevlevi Order after Mevlana*, p.416

This delicious pilav really does live up to its name 'Hassaten Lokma' (Exceptional Lokma).

Serves 5 or more
— 300g or 1 ½ cups long grain rice
— 600ml or 1 pint warm water and 1 tbsp salt for soaking the rice

— 500g or 2 ¼ cups lamb cut into small chunks
— ½ tsp salt
— 125g or ½ cup clarified butter
— 3 onions sliced
— 1 tbsp pine nuts
— 250g or 2 cups carrots cut into 3mm wide matchsticks
— 75g or 1 cup boiled chick peas
— 1 tbsp currants soaked in water for 30 minutes
— ½ tsp ground cinnamon
— ½ tsp ground cloves
— ½ tsp ground cardamom
— 1 tsp salt
— 200g or 1 ½ cups chestnuts, scored, half grilled and peeled
— 600ml or 2 ½ cups hot meat stock (see p. 52)

Soak the rice in hand-hot salted water and set aside until the water has completely cooled.

Wash the meat and fry in a saucepan until it has reabsorbed all its juices.

Add the salt.

In a separate saucepan melt the fat. Add the onions and pine nuts and fry until the onions have turned golden brown. Add the carrots and fry until they have reabsorbed all the juices they release. Add the chick peas, currants, spices and salt and remove from heat. Add the chestnuts and mix into the meat.

Wash the rice several times until the water runs clear. Place a layer of carrots and meat in the bottom of the saucepan. Top with a layer of rice, then with another layer of carrots and meat, another layer of rice and so on. Place a flat plate or lid on top to ensure the layers are kept separate. Trickle the boiling meat stock slowly down the sides of the plate. Cover the saucepan. When it comes to a boil turn the heat down to low. Once it has absorbed all the liquid and formed small craters remove the plate or lid from inside. Cover the mouth of the saucepan with greased paper or a tea towel and replace the lid. Keep on a very low heat for 20 minutes. You may also use a heat diffuser.

Place a dish over the saucepan, tip upside-down and serve.

Köfte for Breaking a Fast

Köfte

'It was told that Celaleddin-i Müstavfi prepared a lavish banquet for iftar [the breaking of the fast] and invited all the most prominent personages. All the guests began to eat with great relish. Mevlana neither ate nor manifested any desire to eat. Müstavfi pressed him to eat, but Mevlana replied apologetically, "My appetite has diminished greatly. It has come to resemble an emaciated animal with a wounded back. Just like an animal, whenever anyone wants to place a saddle on its back it brays and collapses, unable to carry its load. Had it not been beaten and crushed it would have eaten a few köftes."'

Eflaki, *The Tales of the Wise 1*, p:381

The köfte mentioned by Eflaki was probably made from very finely chopped or pounded meat. These days in Konya it is made with minced meat and served at iftar gatherings with onions with sumach. For the sake of convenience, you may also prepare this köfte with minced meat. Nowadays we also add cayenne pepper and thyme to the köfte rather than cinnamon. (I suggest you also add 1 tsp cinnamon.) In the past dry köfte was also the ideal food for taking on journeys.

Serves 5 or more. For the köfte
— 500g or 1lb 2oz lean leg of lamb, pounded or minced twice
— 100g or 1 cup stale breadcrumbs
— 1 large onion, grated
— 1 egg
— ½ tsp ground cumin
— ½ tsp ground black pepper
— ½ tsp salt

For frying the köftes
— 1 tbsp plain flour
— 250g or 1 cup clarified butter or olive oil

Place the meat, breadcrumbs and onions in a bowl. Add the egg, spices and salt and knead for 10 minutes. Form köftes the size and width of an index finger. Heat the fat; coat the köftes in flour and fry. Serve hot accompanied by onions with sumach (see glossary).

Duck with Clarified Butter

Muineddin Pervane's son-in-law, Mecdeddin Atabek, requested Mevlana to allow him to perform a çile [a forty-day period of retirement and fasting]. Mevlana consented. He retired to a cell in the madrasah. A few days later, because Mecdeddin was accustomed to a life of indulgence and comfort, his hunger triumphed. He had a confidant with him who was in the same situation as himself. The two of them agreed to find some way of satisfying their hunger. One night they left their cells, went to one of their friends' houses and explained how hungry they were. The friend prepared a duck with clarified butter and pilav with pepper for them. They both ate heartily and returned to lock themselves in their cells. The following morning, as was his custom, Hazret-i Mevlana went to the cell and, after placing his holy fingers on the door, sniffed them and said 'How strange! This cell does not smell of asceticism but of duck and rice. A disciple must surrender himself to a mature sheikh so the sheikh can watch over every one of his concerns and help him attain his goal.' Whereupon the two friends came out of their cell, fell to Mevlana's feet and begged him to forgive them for their sins.'

Eflaki, *The Book of the Wise 1*, p:257

Biberli Pilav (Rice with Pepper) is similar to the iç pilav prepared nowadays. For this reason I have added cinnamon as well as black pepper. If you wish, you may fry almonds, chopped duck's liver and finely chopped onions, one at a time, and mix them into the pilav with the spices.

Serves 5 or more

— 1 duck
— 2 litres or 8 cups water
— 1 tsp salt

For the pilav with pepper
— 600g or 3 cups long grain rice
— 1.2 litres or 5 cups warm water and 2 tbsps salt for soaking the rice 800ml or 3 ⅓ cups duck stock
— Salt to taste
— 1 tsp ground cinnamon
— 1 tsp black pepper
— 300g or 1 ⅓ cups clarified butter (see glossary)
— 250g or 1 cup clarified butter (for browning the duck)

Trim and wash the duck and place it on to heat in a saucepan with the water. When it comes to a boil skim off the foam that forms on the surface and cover with a lid. Cook on a medium heat for approximately one hour, until the duck is tender. Add salt and remove from heat after ten minutes. Place the duck in a sieve and reserve the stock.

Soak the rice in warm salty water until the water has completely cooled.

Wash several times until the water runs clear. Drain.

Heat the duck stock with salt. When it comes to a boil add the rice and spices and cover. Cook for 3 minutes on high heat, 3 minutes on medium heat and 10 minutes on low heat until all the water has been absorbed. Heat the butter in a frying pan, drizzle over the pilav and place on a very low heat. Cover the saucepan with greased paper and a lid. Keep on a very low heat for 20 minutes. Remove and arrange on a dish.

Heat the second quantity of butter in a frying pan and brown the duck, turning occasionally. Place on top of the rice and serve.

SELECTED RECIPES FROM ALI EŞREF DEDE'S 'FOOD TREATISE'

Soups

Fish Soup

Serves 4

— 75g or ¾ cup ground dehusked wheat
— 1.2 litres or 5 cups water
— 250g or 9oz sea bass
— ½ tsp saffron, soaked overnight in 2 tbsps water
— 50ml or ¼ cup olive oil
— 1 onion
— 5 tbsps chopped fresh mint
— 5 tbsps chopped fresh parsley
— 100ml or ½ cup wine vinegar and 200ml or 1 cup water
— Salt to taste
— 1 egg yolk
— 50ml or ¼ cup lemon juice

— ½ tsp cinnamon
— ½ tsp cinnamon (to garnish)

Wash the wheat and soak in water overnight. In the morning boil for approximately one hour, until the wheat becomes thick and soupy. Strain into a saucepan. If the thickened wheat stock has evaporated, top up with water to get 1 litre or 1 ¾ pints.

Fry the onion in the olive oil until golden brown. Add the mint and parsley and stir, then add the vinegar mixed with 200ml water and the salt. When it comes to the boil, turn the heat down to low and cook for 15–20 minutes. Strain into a saucepan. Place the fish in the strained liquid and boil for approximately 15–20 minutes, until the fish is cooked. Strain, setting aside the liquid. Remove the skin and bones from the fish and divide into several pieces.

Place the dehusked wheat mixture in a saucepan, stirring continuously.

When it comes to a boil, add the fish stock and boil.

Beat the egg yolk in a bowl. Take a little of the soup stock and blend into the yolk, then stir the beaten egg yolk into the soup. When it has come to the boil a couple of times, add the lemon juice. When it boils again, strain the saffron, add the liquid to the soup and remove from the heat immediately. Add the fish and cinnamon and set aside for six hours. Heat the soup on a low flame (to prevent the fish from disintegrating) and ladle into soup bowls. Serve sprinkled with cinnamon.

Liver Soup

Serves 4

- 250g or 9 oz sheep's or lamb's liver
- 200ml or 1 cup water for boiling the liver
- 2 tbsps clarified butter
- 1 litre or 4 cups meat stock
- 50ml or ¼ cup wine vinegar
- 2 egg yolks
- 1 tbsp chopped fresh parsley
- 1 tbsp chopped fresh mint
- ½ tsp cayenne pepper
- ½ tsp cinnamon
- Lemon juice or vinegar

Place the liver in boiling water, boil for 5 minutes and put into a sieve. When it is cool enough to handle, chop finely and fry in the hot butter.

Boil the meat stock. Add the chopped liver. When it comes to a boil add the vinegar. Beat the egg yolks and mix into the soup gradually. Cook for 5–10 minutes, until the smell of raw egg disappears. Add the parsley and mint and bring to the boil. Transfer to a soup tureen, sprinkle with cayenne pepper and cinnamon and serve with lemon juice or vinegar.

Chick Pea Soup

Serves 4

- 150g or 1 cup chick peas
- 600ml or 3 ⅓ cups water for soaking 1
- litre or 4 cups water for boiling
- 800ml or 3 ⅓ cups chicken stock
- Salt to taste
- 1 tsp mint or cayenne pepper
- 4 slices of bread, cut into small cubes

Soak the chick peas in water overnight. In the morning remove the outer skins, place in a saucepan and boil in 1 litre of water for approximately 50 minutes, until the chick peas are tender. Strain. Push the chick peas through a metal sieve (alternatively you can use a blender). Add the chicken stock and return to the heat, stirring continuously. When it comes to a boil turn the heat down to low. Cook for a further 10–15 minutes, stirring occasionally. Brown the croûtons in the oven (you may also fry them in butter). Ladle the soup into bowls, sprinkle with mint or cayenne pepper and serve with the croûtons.

Meat

Butcher's Kebab

Serves 5 or more

- 250g or 1 cup minced lamb
- 250g or 9oz lamb's liver, chopped very finely
- 100g or 1 cup breadcrumbs
- 1 very finely chopped onion
- 150g or ¾ cup long grain rice
- ½ tsp black pepper
- ¼ tsp cayenne pepper
- ¼ tsp cinnamon
- ½ tsp ground aniseed
- ¼ tsp dried mint
- ½ tsp salt
- 200ml or 1 cup water
- 1 bunch parsley, chopped
- 1 egg
- 1 sheet of caul fat (see glossary)

Knead all the ingredients together. Wash the caul fat, dip it into warm water, remove it and spread it out on a tray. Place the köfte mixture inside and use the caul fat to wrap it up into a large bundle. Cook for 30–40 minutes in a preheated oven at 175°C. Turn out upside-down into a dish and serve.

Grilled Lamb Cutlets

Lamb Külbastı

Serves 4

- ½ kg or 1lb 2oz leg of lamb (pounded with a meat mallet)
- Salt to taste
- 10 cloves garlic, peeled
- 400ml or 1 ¾ cups meat stock
- ¼ glass wine vinegar
- ½ tsp black pepper
- ½ tsp ground cumin 4–5 cloves
- 3–4 pieces of mastic gum (ground with a pinch of salt) (see glossary)
- ½ tsp cinnamon

Sprinkle the meat with salt. Brown both sides on a brazier, then place inside a casserole dish. Add the garlic, meat stock, vinegar, pepper and cumin, and cover. When it comes to a boil turn the heat down to low. Cook for approximately 30 minutes, until the meat becomes tender. Add the cloves and the ground mastic. Cook for another 10 minutes. Sprinkle with cinnamon and serve in the casserole dish.

Dry Köfte

Serves 4

- 250g or 1 cup minced lamb
- ¼ tsp black pepper
- ¼ tsp cayenne pepper

— ¼ tsp ground cardamoms
— ¼ tsp cinnamon Salt to taste

Knead all the ingredients thoroughly. Form into flat, oval köftes. Place a metal bowl full of water inside a steel casserole dish and arrange the köftes inside the casserole dish, around the edges of the bowl of water. Cover and cook for 25–30 minutes. Alternatively half fill the casserole dish with water, place the köftes in a metal bowl in the dish, cover and cook.

Milk Kebab

Serves 4

— 250g or 9oz leg of lamb or mutton cut into small chunks
— ⅛ tsp salt
— ⅛ tsp black pepper
— ⅛ tsp cayenne pepper
— 400ml or 1 ¾ cups boiling milk
— strong plain flour
— Cinnamon to taste

Mix the meat with the spices and set aside for 3–4 hours. Place in a saucepan. Pour the hot milk on top and put on to heat. When it comes to a boil turn the heat down to low, simmer for 10 minutes.

Place the meat in a sieve. Reserve the strained milk.

When the meat has cooled, thread it on to skewers. Heat the milk used for cooking the meat. Place the skewers on a barbecue 10cm above the coals. As the kebabs dry out brush them with some of the hot milk. When fat from the cooking meat starts to drip on to the coals, sprinkle a very small amount of strong plain flour on the meat. Once the kebabs are nicely browned, arrange the skewers on a dish and sprinkle with cinnamon. Serve with rice pilav (see p. 105).

Lamb Casserole Cooked Upside-Down

Tas Kebab

You may also like to arrange the rice around the upside-down tas (wide metal bowl) and remove the tas at the table.

Serves 5 or more

- 1 kg or 2 ¼ lb heavily marbled mutton or lamb cut into small chunks
- 500g or 1lb 2oz onions, finely chopped
- 10 cloves garlic
- 3 tbsps finely chopped fresh parsley
- 3 tbsps finely chopped fresh mint
- ½ tsp cayenne pepper
- ½ tsp black pepper
- ½ tsp ground cinnamon
- ½ tsp ground cardamom
- 1 tsp ground aniseed
- ½ tsp salt

Mix all the ingredients together in a bowl. Set aside for 4–5 hours. Put into a metal casserole dish large enough and place upside-down in the centre of a deep baking tin. Place a heavy weight on top. Place on the hob on a low heat. (This will release the juices and let them be reabsorbed.)

After approximately two hours, when all the liquid has been completely absorbed, lift off the tas and serve with Rice Pilav (see p. 105).

Offal

Liver Kebab

Serves 4

— 250g or 9oz sheep's or lamb's liver cut into small cubes
— Caul fat as required (see glossary)
— 5 cloves garlic
— Salt to taste
— ¼ cup wine vinegar

Thread the cubes of liver on to skewers. Wrap them with the caul fat. Place 10cm above the coals on a barbecue and cook for 3–4 minutes on one side, then turn over and cook the other side in the same way. Remove the caul fat and place the liver in a warmed dish.

Crush the garlic with the salt, add the vinegar and drizzle over the liver. Cover and allow to steep for 5 minutes on a very low heat. If you like you may add a spoonful of clarified butter to the vinegar and a little meat stock and cook for a few more minutes. Arrange in a dish and serve.

Poultry

Grilled Chicken Casserole

Chicken Külbastı

Serves 4

— ½ kg or 1lb 2oz chicken thighs
— ½ tsp salt
— ½ tsp cayenne pepper
— 400ml or 1 ¾ cups meat stock
— Rice or bulgur pilav

Debone the chicken thighs and divide the chicken into egg-sized pieces approximately 1cm thick. Make slits on one side with a knife, rub with salt and pepper and set aside for three hours. Cook each side for 5 minutes on a barbecue 10cm above the coals, then transfer to a shallow cooking pan or casserole dish. Pour on the boiling meat stock, cover and cook for another 10–15 minutes. Arrange on a plate and serve with rice or bulgur pilav.

Seafood

Swordfish Collar Casserole

Serves 4

— 800g or 1lb 12oz swordfish fillets (4 pieces)

— Salt to taste
— 200ml or 1 cup olive oil
— 4 heads garlic, peeled and separated into cloves
— 1 bunch of unripe grapes (koruk)
— 100ml or ½ glass verjuice (may be substituted with lemon juice if verjuice is unavailable)

Wash and salt the fish, drain in a sieve, heat the oil and fry. In a shallow dish place alternate layers of fish, garlic and unripe grapes. Add the verjuice and cover. Cook on a low heat for approximately 20–25 minutes, until the garlic is soft.

Arrange on a dish and serve.

Vegetables

Stuffed Aubergines

Aleppo Dolma

Serves 4
— 750g or 1lb 10oz aubergines

For the stuffing
— 250g or 1 cup minced meat
— 1 finely chopped onion
— 2 fresh, long green chillies, finely chopped
— 50g or 1 cup chopped aubergine pulp
— 75g or ⅓ cup long grain rice, washed

- 100ml or ½ cup water
- ¼ tsp ground cinnamon
- ¼ tsp ground cardamom
- ¼ tsp dried mint
- ¼ tsp saffron
- Salt to taste
- ½ kg sheep's or lamb's ribs, divided into hand-sized pieces
- 400ml or 1 ¾ cups hot water
- 2 tbsps sour pomegranate juice (see glossary) or verjuice to taste

Peel one or two of the aubergines and divide them into half-centimetre thick slices to serve as lids for the dolma. Cut the tops off the remaining aubergines, cut them in half widthwise and scoop out the pulp. Soak the aubergine pulp and aubergine slices in salted water for 15–20 minutes. Chop the pulp very finely and reserve 50g or 1 cup to mix with the stuffing.

Mix the minced meat, onions, chillies, chopped aubergine pulp, rice and spices together and stuff the hollowed-out aubergines with the mixture. Place an aubergine slice on top of each stuffed aubergine.

Arrange the ribs at the bottom of the saucepan and place the dolmas between them. Mix the water and sour pomegranate juice, pour over the meat and dolmas and put on to heat. When it comes to a boil turn the heat down to low. Cook for 50–60 minutes. Arrange the meat and the dolma in a dish and serve.

Butternut Squash with Meat and Onions

Butternut Squash Kalye

Serves 4

— ½ kg or 1lb 2oz butternut squash
— ½ kg or 1lb 2oz fatty lamb chopped, using the bıçak arası technique (see glossary)
— 2 onions, finely chopped
— ½ tsp cayenne pepper
— ½ tsp cinnamon
— ½ tsp black pepper
— Salt to taste
— 100ml or ½ cup verjuice (or, if unavailable, wine vinegar)
— 200ml or ¾ cup water
— 100ml or ½ cup of grape juice (if unavailable, 1 tbsp honey or pekmez or sugar)
— 4 cloves garlic, crushed with 1 tbsp water, then strained
— 1 tsp dried mint
— 1 tsp dried mint (to garnish)

Wash and peel the butternut squash, cut into large pieces, strain.

Mix the meat, onions, spices and salt. Place alternate layers of butternut squash and meat in a saucepan. Add the verjuice and water, cover and put on to heat. When it comes to a boil turn the heat down to low. After 60 minutes add the grape juice, juice from the strained garlic and the mint. Cook for another 15–20 minutes.

Arrange on a dish, sprinkle with dried mint and serve.

Fried Aubergines with Vinegar

Aubergine Paça

If you prefer, you can use sliced onions instead of garlic for this recipe.

Serves 4

— ½ kg or 1lb 2oz aubergines
— 300ml or 1 ¼ cups water and 1 tbsp salt for soaking 2 cups of olive oil
— 50g or ½ cup plain flour 200ml or 1 cup wine vinegar 4 cloves garlic
— ¼ tsp salt
— 1 tbsp of the oil used for frying the aubergines

Wash, peel and slice the aubergines. Place them in salted water for 20 minutes, rinse thoroughly and drain. Heat the oil. Coat the aubergines in flour and fry. Arrange in a casserole dish.

Crush the garlic with the salt, beat with the vinegar and the tablespoon of oil from the fried aubergines, pour over the aubergines. Put on to heat. When they begin to sizzle turn the heat right down to very low and allow to cook for 25–30 minutes.

Purslane Omelette with Fried Meat

Serves 4

— ½ kg or 1lb 2oz purslane
— 50g or 4 tbsps clarified butter 1 onion, finely chopped
— 3 eggs

— Salt to taste
— 1 tbsp clarified butter (for the frying pan)
— ½ serving kavurma (see p: 156)

Trim, wash, chop and drain the purslane.

Fry the onion in the clarified butter. Add the purslane and continue to fry until all the juices have been reabsorbed. Beat the eggs in a bowl and add the purslane and salt. Put the tablespoon of clarified butter in a frying pan. When hot, pour in the egg mixture. When it has browned, flip over and brown the other side. Turn out into a large plate. Heat the kavurma, arrange on top of the purslane omelette and serve.

Fruit

Stuffed Melon

Melon Dolma

Serves 4

— 8 kelek (unripe melons the size of oranges)
— 250g or 1 cup minced meat
— 2 tbsps clarified butter or butter
— 2 onions, finely chopped
— 75g or ⅓ cup long grain rice, washed
— 75g or ½ cup blanched almonds
— 75g or ½ cup pine nuts
— ½ tsp cinnamon

— ¼ tsp cayenne pepper
— ½ tsp ground coriander
— ½ tsp salt
— 400ml or 3 ⅓ cups hot water

Slice off the top of the melons and set aside to use as lids. Remove the seeds, wash and drain.

Place the minced meat in a frying pan and put on to heat. When it is half fried add the clarified butter and the onions and fry. Stir in the rice, almonds, pine nuts, spices and salt. Stuff the melons with this mixture. Replace the lids on the melons and secure with a cocktail stick. Arrange in a baking tin. Pour the water over the top. Bake in a preheated oven at 175°C for 40–50 minutes. If you are using a hob, cook for 50–60 minutes.

Salads

Caviar Salad

Serves 4

— 50g or ½ cup fish roe (carp or any other fish roe)
— 2 onions, grated
— 50ml or ½ cup olive oil

In a bowl, beat all the ingredients together thoroughly with a wooden spoon to achieve a paste-like consistency. Strain through a fine sieve or wide gauze. Arrange on a dish and serve.

Lettuce Salad

Serves 4

— 8 lettuce leaves
— 1 bunch fresh mint leaves
— 1 bunch fresh parsley
— 1 bunch wild radish leaves (if available)
— 100ml or ½ cup vinegar
— ½ tsp salt
— 100ml or ½ cup olive oil
— Roses, judas tree blossom or quince blossom, depending on the season

Wash the vegetables and drain to remove excess liquid. Chop roughly and place in a large bowl.

Mix the vinegar with the salt and pour on to the salad, followed by the olive oil. Strain carefully, reserving the strained dressing, then pour over the salad a second time. Repeat this procedure a few times, not only to prevent the salad from wilting but also to ensure that the vinegar coats all the leaves. Decorate the salad with the flowers and serve.

Sardine Salad

Ali Eşref Dede writes that sardines were caught during the summer and preserved by salting and that they were called pickles in the vicinity of Istanbul and the islands. He also indicates that two types of sardines came from Europe in small glass jars, one called sardines, the other anchovies, and that there was no difference between them in taste. You may use either preserved sardines or anchovies for this salad.

Serves 4

— 100g or ½ cup salted sardines
— 100ml or ½ cup wine vinegar 1 onion
— 5 tbsps finely chopped fresh parsley
— 50ml or ¼ cup olive oil
— 50ml or ¼ cup lemon juice or vinegar

Wash the salted fish and marinate in 100ml or ½ cup vinegar for one hour. Remove the scales, head and tail and return to the marinade for a further 30 minutes.

Slice the onions very thinly, mix with the parsley and spread out on a dish.

Arrange the fish on top.

Beat the olive oil and 50ml or ¼ cup vinegar or lemon juice in a bowl until it turns white. Pour over the fish and serve.

Rice and Pasta

Bulgur Pilav with Chestnuts

Serves 4

— 10–15 chesnuts
— 2 tbsp currants
— 300g or 1 ½ cups bulgur wheat
— 600ml or 2 ½ cups meat stock (see p. 52)
— ½ tsp salt
— 200g or 1 cup clarified butter (see glossary)
— ½ tsp cinnamon

Score the chestnuts with a knife and roast over a flame until the shell can be removed. Divide them into 2 or 3 pieces. Remove the stalks from the currants and wash them.

Place the bulgur wheat, chestnuts and currants in a saucepan.

Boil the meat stock with the salt and pour over the bulgur, chestnuts and currants, and cover. Cook for 3 minutes on a high heat, 5 minutes on a medium heat, then continue to cook on a low heat until the bulgur has absorbed all the water and formed small craters. Heat the clarified butter in a frying pan and drizzle over the bulgur pilav. Sprinkle with the cinnamon and allow to steep on a very low heat for 20 minutes. Arrange on a dish and serve with chicken külbastı and yogurt.

Aubergine Pilav

In Ali Eşref Dede's recipe the aubergines are boiled. However, if you fry the aubergines without boiling them first they will be firmer.

Serves 4

— 300g or 1 ½ cups long grain rice
— 400ml or 1 ¾ cups warm water and 1 tbsp salt, for soaking the rice
— 250g or 9oz aubergine
— 400ml or 1 ¾ cups water and ½ tsp salt, for boiling the aubergines
— 50ml or ¼ cup olive oil
— 1 onion, finely chopped
— 400ml or 1 ¾ cups water
— 50ml or ¼ cup of olive oil
— ½ tsp salt
— 2 pieces mastic gum (see glossary)
— ½ tsp cinnamon
— ¼ tsp saffron
— ⅛ tsp cayenne pepper
— ⅛ tsp black pepper

Soak the rice in warm salted water until the water has completely cooled. Peel the aubergines and cut into small cubes. Blanch for 2 minutes in enough boiling salted water just to cover them. Drain.

Fry the onions in the olive oil until they begin to turn golden brown. Add the aubergines and stir. Fry until they colour, then set aside. Wash the rice in several changes of water until the water runs clear. Place in a saucepan. Add the olive oil, salt and boiling water.

Crush the mastic gum in a mortar with a pinch of salt and add to the rice, together with the cinnamon, pepper and saffron. Cover and cook for 3 minutes on a high heat, 2 minutes on a medium heat and 10 minutes on a low heat, until it has absorbed all the liquid. Mix in the aubergines and onions. Cover the top of the saucepan with greased paper, replace the lid and allow to steep on the lowest possible heat (you may also use a heat diffuser) for 20 minutes. Arrange the rice on a dish and serve.

Pilav without Fat

Serves 5 or more

— 1 kg or 2 ¼ lb chicken
— 1 litre or 4 cups water
— 300g or 1 ½ cups of long grain rice
— Salt to taste
— 400ml or 1 ¾ cups warm water and 1 tbsp salt, for soaking the rice
— 900ml or 3 ¾ cups stock from the boiled chicken
— ½ tsp salt
— 3–4 pieces mastic gum crushed with ½ tsp salt
— 1 tsp cinnamon

Boil the chicken in the water. When it is cooked, add salt and cook for a further 10 minutes. Remove from the heat. Strain the chicken into a sieve set over a large bowl or saucepan. Reserve

500ml or 18 fl oz chicken stock for the pilav. Shred the meat from the chicken and put into the remaining chicken stock.

Pick over the rice and pour enough warm salted water over it to completely cover it. Soak until the water has cooled, then wash several times and drain.

Place the chicken stock in a saucepan together with the salt, crushed mastic chewing gum and cinnamon. When it comes to a boil add the rice and cover with a lid. When it begins to boil cook for 3 minutes on a high heat, 3 minutes on a medium heat and approximately 10 minutes on a low heat until it has absorbed all the liquid and formed small craters. Cover with greased paper and a lid and allow to steep on a very low heat (you may also use a heat diffuser) for 20 minutes.

While the pilav is steeping bring the shredded chicken pieces and stock to a boil once, to heat the chicken, and strain. Once drained, mix into the pilav. Alternatively, transfer the pilav to a dish, arrange the chicken pieces on top and serve.

Börek

Leek Börek

Onion börek is prepared in the same way, although the filling is prepared slightly differently. Fry only the onions in the fat and add the eggs.

Serves 5 or more For the filling
— ½ kg or 1lb 2oz leeks
— 2 onions, chopped
— 4 tbsps clarified butter
— 2 eggs
— 150g or 1 cup feta cheese

For the pastry
— 1 egg
— 1 tbsp clarified butter, melted, or olive oil
— 100ml or ½ cup water or water with ashes (see p. 117)
— 100ml or ½ cup milk
— Salt to taste
— 300g or 2 ½ cups half strong plain, half self-raising flour
— 100g or 1 cup plain flour, for rolling out
— 250g or 1 cup melted clarified butter, for drizzling over the pastry
— 125g or ½ cup clarified butter, to brush the pastry

Wash, trim and finely slice the leeks. Cook in boiling water for 15 minutes and strain. Fry the onions in the clarified butter, add the leeks and continue to fry.

Break the eggs into the frying pan and stir until they solidify. Remove from heat and add the cheese.

Combine the oil, milk, salt and flour to make a soft, pliable dough. Divide into 12 walnut-sized pieces and allow to stand under a damp cloth for 30 minutes. Roll each piece out into a very thin sheet. Grease a baking tin and line with the first sheet. Drizzle a spoonful of melted clarified butter over the top and place a second sheet over it. Repeat this process with eight sheets of pastry. Add the filling. Top with the remaining four sheets of pastry, drizzling a spoonful of melted clarified butter over each, as before.

Heat the 125g clarified butter. Brush the top of the börek so as not to leave any area uncovered. Bake in a preheated oven at 200°C for approximately 30 minutes. When you remove it from the oven, cover with another tray to prevent it from drying out and wrap with a large cloth.

Chicken Börek

Serves 5 or more For the filling

— 1 kg or 2 ¼ lb chicken, boiled and shredded
— 3 onions, sliced
— ½ tsp salt
— 2 tbsps clarified butter

For the pastry

— 1 serving of leek börek pastry

Mix the onions with the salt and set aside for five minutes. Rub the salt in, then wash and squeeze well to eliminate any excess liquid. Fry onions in the hot clarified butter until they have turned a golden colour. Add the chicken, stir once or twice and remove from the heat. Proceed as for leek börek, substituting the chicken filling for the leeks.

یا حضرت مولانا

Sweets

Kadayıf with Almonds and Gold Vark

Kadayıf Mücver

Ali Eşref Dede's kadayıf mücver, decorated with gold vark (incredibly fine gold foil), is one of the exceptional dishes of Mevlevi cuisine. There is a similar sweet in Melceü Tabbahin, called Katife, prepared without gold vark, resembling şehriye pilav (pilav with fried, then boiled, vermicelli): 'It's called Katife, or künife, and is famous in Arabia. Separate fine kadayıf strands by hand, cook in a saucepan or baking tin with clarified butter for a while. Add sugar or honey and cook for a little longer, stirring with a spoon. Arrange in a plate or copper dish, as with şehriye pilav, and serve.' It will taste even better if you add pistachio nuts. Ali Eşref Dede shapes the sweet in a mücver pan with small craters. As his recipe is very complicated, I have adapted it to make it easier to prepare. Dede mentions that the walnut and almond varieties are prepared with honey syrup. I am giving both versions, although I prefer the syrupy variety.

Serves 4

— 250g tel kadayıf (see p. 126)
— 125g or ½ cup butter
— 40g or ¼ cup finely chopped almonds
— 40g or ¼ cup finely chopped pistachio nuts
— 40g or ¼ cup icing sugar (or according to taste)
— 4 sheets gold vark

Separate the strands of kadayıf by hand and place in a deep baking tin. Half cook on a low heat, spreading the kadayıf out in the tray from time to time and turning it over. Mix the sugar and nuts in with the kadayıf. Cook, stirring with a spoon, until it starts to brown. Spoon into individual bowls, pressing down firmly, then place a plate over the top and turn upside-down. Top each kadayıf with a sheet of gold vark and serve.

Kadayıf Mücver with Syrup

This syrup should be poured over the sweet just before serving.

For the syrup
— 150g or ⅔ cup caster sugar
— 200ml or 1 cup water

For the kadayıf mücver
— 250g tel kadayıf (see p. 126)
— 125g or ½ cup butter
— 40g or ¼ cup finely chopped almonds
— 40g or ¼ cup finely chopped walnuts

Put the sugar and water in a saucepan to heat. When it comes to the boil turn the heat down. Simmer for two minutes and remove from heat.

Prepare the kadayıf as in the previous recipe and arrange on a plate. Spoon the hot but not boiling syrup over the kadayıf, without spoiling its shape or leaving any parts uncovered. Top with gold vark and serve.

Pine Nut Compote

Pine Nut Hoşaf

Serves 4

- 150g or 1 cup pine nuts
- 800ml or 3 ⅓ cups water
- 150g or ½ cup sugar or honey
- 100ml or ½ cup rose water
- 1 tsp roasted pine nuts, to garnish

Dry roast the pine nuts for the garnish in the oven or in a frying pan on the hob until they begin to turn golden brown. Heat the sugar or honey and water, bring to the boil and remove from the heat immediately.

Crush the 150g pine nuts in a stone mortar together with the rose water and a little water. Adding the syrup a little at a time, crush completely, add the remaining syrup and pour into a serving bowl. Sprinkle with the roasted pine nuts.

Orange Compote

Orange Hoşaf

Serves 5 or more

- 200ml or 1 cup orange juice
- 400ml or 1 ¾ cups water
- 450g or 2 cups caster sugar
- Orange slices (approximately 20)

Put the orange juice, water and sugar on to heat. When it comes to a boil turn the heat down, simmer for 2 minutes and remove from the heat. While the hoşaf is boiling, peel the oranges, remove the pith, slice and arrange in a bowl. Pour the boiled hoşaf over them and serve chilled.

Pistachio Compote

Pistachio Hoşaf

Serves 4

— 150g or 1 cup shelled, peeled pistachio nuts
— 800ml or 3 ⅓ cups water
— 150g or ⅔ cup caster sugar
— 100ml or 1 cup rose water
— 1 tbsp pistachios, to garnish

Put the sugar and water on to heat in a saucepan. Bring to the boil and remove from the heat.

Crush the pistachios in a stone mortar with the rose water and a little water. Crush completely, adding the syrup gradually. Add the remaining syrup and transfer to a bowl. Sprinkle with whole pistachios.

Drinks

Sweet Almond Juice with Rosewater

Almond Herpere

Serves 4

— 150g or 1 cup almonds
— 200ml or 1 cup water 900ml or 3 ¾ cups water
— 75g or ⅓ cup caster sugar (or according to taste)
— 100ml or ½ cup rosewater
— Ground cinnamon

Pound the almonds in a mortar, crush with water. Strain through fine gauze and extract the milk. Crush the solid particles remaining in the gauze again with water and strain through the gauze. Combine the almond milk, water, sugar and rosewater. Put on to heat, stirring continuously. When it comes to a boil lower the heat and simmer for 10–15 minutes. Pour into glasses, sprinkle with cinnamon and serve. Almond herpere can be served hot or cold.

Rosewater and Lemon Drink

Pelteşin

Serves 4

— 800ml or 3 ⅓ cups water
— 4 tsps cornstarch
— 4 tbsps caster sugar
— 100ml or ½ cup rosewater
— 2 tbsps lemon juice

Mix the water, cornstarch and rosewater together and put on to heat. Boil for 5 minutes. When it begins to thicken turn the heat down and add the lemon juice. Bring to the boil once again, pour into glasses and serve.

Preserved Foods

Homemade Pasta

Erişte

In Konya erişte is prepared and kept to be used in winter. When prepared in this way it is called 'erişte pilav' and can also be used to make the dessert resembling macaroni pudding known as milky selemen.

— 2 eggs
— 1 eggshell full of water

— 200g or 1 ¾ cups flour
— ½ tsp salt

For boiling the erişte:
— 500ml or 2 ½ cups water
— 1 tsp salt
— 1 tsp olive oil

For cooking
— 150g or 2 cups erişte
— 3 tbsps clarified butter
— 150g or 1 cup feta cheese, crumbled
— ¼ glass parsley, chopped

Combine the eggs, water and salt in a bowl. Add the flour and knead for 15–20 minutes until you have a firm dough. Divide into two pieces and allow to rest under a damp cloth for 30 minutes.

Roll out with a rolling pin to the thickness of a knife blade (3mm). Set aside on a cloth and wait for it to dry slightly. Cut the dough into strips 4cm wide. Place 4 or 5 strips one on top of the other. Using a sharp knife, cut strips 3mm wide. Leave on a cloth to dry for 1–2 days, mixing occasionally.

To cook erişte
Boil the water with the salt and olive oil. Add the erişte. When it comes to a boil turn down the heat and cover. Cook for 20 minutes, drain. Rinse with cold water and return to the saucepan.

Heat the clarified butter in a frying pan. Pour on to the erişte and cover. Leave for 10 minutes on a very low heat, transfer to a dish, sprinkle with the feta cheese and, if liked, the parsley, and serve.

Pickled Turnips

'Whenever Baha Veled's disciple, Hazret-i Seyyid-i Sırdan, desired pickles, he would say, "Turnip pickles are good for you and, of all the pickles, they are the best. Eating raw turnip improves the eyesight." Hazreti Seyyid was pre-eminent in the science of medicine.'
Eflaki, *The Tales of the Wise*, p:119

— ½ kg or 1lb 2oz turnip
— 1 litre or 4 cups water
— ½ tsp salt
— 5–6 chick peas
— 2 ½ litres or 10 cups wine vinegar
— 1 tbsp pekmez (grape syrup)
— ½ tsp salt

Trim and wash the turnips and cut them into slices. Boil the salt and water, add the turnips. When it comes to the boil again, turn the heat down, boil for two minutes and strain. Wash the chick peas and put them into a jar. Add the strained turnips. Blend the vinegar, pekmez and salt together. Pour into the jar so as to completely cover the turnips. Store in a cool dry place until they are ready to eat – about three weeks.

SELECTED COUPLETS FROM MEVLANA'S WORKS RELATED TO FOOD AND DRINK

Nourishment

'The true nourishment of humans is God's light.
Animal nourishment is unbefitting for them.' M2:172-C:1085

'That is the nourishment of pure mortals blessed with riches,
eaten without mouth or implements.' M2:173-C:1088

'Every friend is food for the heart, all knowledge purification.'
M2:173-C:1091

'The food of life is divine light; life does not develop
and grow with any other nutriment.' M4:278-C:1955

*'Were I to die and lie in a coffin my food would still be your love;
I am human in appearance, human in form,
but it is angels' nutriment that feeds me.'* D2:122-C:990

Agriculture

*'Spring rain pampers, enriches, cultivates the vineyard, the garden,
while autumn rain yellows and fades it.'* M1:389-C:2048

*'The sower of grain soon has an empty bin
but the benefits become clear in the field.'* M:408-C:2248

*'"Become a crop", He commands and turns me green,
"Turn ugly", He commands, and turns me yellow.'* M:443-C:2473

'Ascetism lies in labouring to sow seeds; talent in their germination.' M6:320-C:2095

Being Hunted

'The falcon too brings prey from the hills, but gliding with its own wings it is hunted; therefore the sultan keeps it with the partridge and the hazel grouse.' M6:700-C:4678

*'Come to your senses, don't lay a trap to snare a rabbit
to find you have hunted a lion.'* D5:245-C:2840

Abstinence/Health

'I have become vinegar blended with honey and found a remedy for liver disorders; I have cured that ill.' M1:595-C:3677

'Abstinence is truly the root of medicine; abstain and observe how it strengthens and invigorates you.' M:486-C:2923

'As long as you feed your body rich, sweet food you will never see its essence grow fat.' M2:69-C:265

'Hoping to reap what you have not sown is a raw hope;
don't eat anything raw (o son). Raw food makes you sick.' 2:126-C:733

'You are honey in this world and the next.
We are vinegar in this world and the next. And as for this bile,
vinegar sherbet with honey will cure it.' M2:285-C:1865

'Those physicians give nourishment, offer fruit to the sick;
these things are strengthening and invigorating for the bestial life.'
M3:325-C:2704

'This contempt is bred from familiarity, as is love;
sickness proceeds from lavish food and drink, as do health and vigour.'
M4:420-C:3011

'Because eating helva out of time makes you bilious.' M6:398-C:2607

'Friends' hearts can be so burdened with grief that no medicine
will cure it. Neither sleeping nor travelling nor eating will alleviate

it. As they say, "a sick man's cure is the face of a friend", he only recovers upon seeing the face of a friend.' FM:338

'It's difficult to play a tambour and make the deaf hear, and to mention sugar to someone with a liver complaint.' D2:2206

'To practise abstinence you deny the sick man helva, you won't wear a kind expression, but you are making your patient grow worse: don't.' D2:398-C:330

Aid

'O rose in the rose garden who resembles the graceful cypress, watch over those who have nothing; give them a loaf of bread, or a hundred, come, be generous to the poor.' D2:147-C:1180

'Give respect, receive respect. Give bread, get bread in return. Be compassion- ate, so you may be treated with compassion, come, be generous to the poor.' D2:147-C:1186

Hospitality

'When you feel a flutter of joy inside, water it. And when it bears fruit offer it to your friends.' M3:51-C:363

'Where is the meat, said the man; there is a guest here; and tables must be laid and food served to guests.' M5:518-C:2

'Visiting a friend empty-handed is like going to a mill without wheat.'
M1:531-C:3183

Love

'The heavens whirl for lovers; this whirling vault of heaven whirls with love, for love. Not for the baker, nor for the blacksmith, nor the carpenter, nor the seller of perfumes. As the heavens whirl for love, come, let us set to whirling too.' D5:145-C:1678,79,80

'Love is like the inner essence, while the world is a shell; love seems like helva, and the world like a cauldron.' D5:73-C:851

'The gardeners of love reap fruit from their own hearts.' D5:175-C:1989

'O love, just as honey and sugar become one in helva, so have you became one with my heart, in my heart.' D5:217-C:2510

'Do not talk too much of love, drink it; speaking is not the same as eating and drinking.' D5:338-C:4174

Wine

'A single drop of divine wine will make the soul renounce both wine and cupbearers.' M3:88-C:823

'God has imbued His wine with such enchantment that the drunk would renounce both worlds for a single drop.' M4:375-C:2683

'There exist wines of blessedness that take the mind up to a point from which it will never again journey.' M4:375-C:2689

*'It is to eliminate grief, sorrow, eradicate anxiety,
give people strength that He made a stream of wine flow from grapes.'*
M5:274-C:1635

'The wine you drink is haram; while we drink nothing but halal.'
M6:112-C:645

'Know that there is dizziness and mental confusion in the wine of death; put down that violet wine, renounce pomegranate wine.'
D3:187-C:1695

'His wine is not of grape juice, nor his goblet of glass, nor his meze, like that of base creatures, of sugar, and almonds.'
D3:336-C:3300

Intoxication

*'Wine was intoxicated with me, not I with wine.
The world took its shape from me, not I from it.'* M1:351-C:1820

'What is drunkenness? It's looking at the tamarisk tree and seeing a sandalwood tree, it's the complete transformation of perceptions.'
M1:262-C: 1206

'What a state of elation my soul would reach, in this vineyard, this garden, this springtime; in this plain, in the tulip garden of this

invisible universe it would become intoxicated and take flight. I would journey without head nor feet; I would eat sweetmeats without lips nor teeth.' M1:394-C:2101–2

*'They drank wine before the creation of grapes,
they became intoxicated and ecstatic.'* M2:62-C:180

'Join the intoxicated souls that even mature minds long for when they drink wine; if you drink, drink as they do.' M3:79-C:711

Meze

*'Ashab-ı Kehf drank of that wine and ate of that meze,
and lost his senses for exactly three hundred and nine years.'*
M4:294-C:2098

*'If your body is drunk on date wine and meze,
be certain that your soul is a stranger to the cluster of the divine universe.'* M5:387-C:2447

*'God is scattering meze after meze, wine upon wine.
Climb up to the mina- ret, recite the sala,[1] and invite everyone to partake.'* M5:395-C:2533

'Know that this world, overflowing with meze and bread, is the crocodile's open mouth.' M6:610-C:4097

*'We are flowers in the garden of the heavens;
we are meze and wine at God's gathering.'* D5:300-C:3573

'The drunken souls smashed the pitchers and sat at the bottom of the fermenting jar. Lord, what wine they drank, what meze they ate.' DI:247-C:2320

Taste

'If reason could fathom this taste, what need would there be for so many miracles.' MI:399-C:2152

'It is certain that every species savours its own kind. Take a look; the half piece relishes its whole self.' MI:218-C:894

'Like bread and water, they too have been transformed into our species and increased our strength.' MI:218-C:894

Sweetness

'Love sweetens bitterness; because the principle of love is to set us on the right path.' MI:455-C:2591

'Many a sweet thing resembles sugar but conceals poison within.' m1:455-c:2595 'The juice of koruk [unripe grapes] is sour, but once that koruk turns into grapes how sweet and lovely it becomes.' MI:456-C:2612

'In the fermenting jar, once again it is bitter, haram; but, as vinegar, what a fine companion for bread!' MI:456-C:2613

'Almond helva fashioned from His walnuts, His almonds, His sugar does not only sweeten my palate, but floods my vision with light.'
D1:108-C:1009

'Let it be sworn to the immaculate essence of God, Master of the nine heav- ens, that death is like a maker of helva who fashions helva with the sugar of reunion with the beloved.' D1:309-C:2858

Salt

'Because that world is like a saltcellar; anything that goes there is drained of colour.' M6:287-C:1860

'Come to your senses, don't rub salt into my wounds; come to your senses, don't put on airs of aggression and, besieged by doubt, drink this poison.' M6:609-C:4083

'A man free from conceit, free from egotism has entered our kitchen, he will take a handful of salt from the saltcellar, cast it at us, and turn us both sweet and savoury.' D2:240-C:1950

'Only the person who eats the dish, puts it into his mouth and chews it is aware of the salt it contains.' D5:482-C:6616

Water

'The sun is wakefulness, while hope is like ice; water is wakefulness, while this world is dirt.' M1:392-C:2077

'Water is above fire in majesty, but place water in a pot and see how fire makes it boil and bubble. Put a cauldron between the two and fire will make that water vanish, transform it into air.' M1:439-C:2438–9

'From this spring I drank sweet, crystalline water; that water refreshed my vision, my soul.' M3:181-C:1413

'Just as a hadji's function is to circumambulate the Kaaba, it is the function of the thirsty person to wander around the spring, roam the river banks, listen to the babbling water.' M4:117-C:753

'The highest heaven is a font of kindness, a font of justice;
beneath it flow four streams brimming with wisdom,
The stream of milk, of eternal honey, of wine,
and of water that flows away: the Tigris.' M5:274-C:1628–9

'He provided everyone with water, that they may be cleansed, and drink their fill.' M5:275-C:1637

'Wash both hands and come and sit at the table; after all, water was created for washing the hands and face.' D3:130-C:1115

Blessed Food

'Go to your last host; leaving your heart in his home will pay for the food you ate there.' M3:46-C:291

'Work is nothing but hardship, toil and sweat; but its payment is pure silver and gold, dish upon dish of food.' M3:413-C:3448

'I want no other food than this; I cannot relinquish this exquisite taste and stoop to the taste of walnuts and sugar.' M4:110-C:687

'Once you start walking you go far, but without feet.
You eat hundreds of delicacies; but without the effort of chewing.'
M4:157-C:1106

'What tasty delicacies rain out of the sky on Christ in Moses' lovely desert, what nourishment, O Lord, what sweets.' D3:33-C:210

'We are pictures created by your artistic hand, nourished with your food, fed on your bread.' D4:228-C:2151

Cooked Dishes (Aş)

'Houris are more beauteous than Bulgarian slave girls,
and the taste of life- giving wine more sumptuous
than that of bulgur aş.' D3:324-C:3160

'My tears, muddied with grief, have made their mark.
The outcome: my face no longer endures sullenness,
nor my bowl base lentil aş.' D4:392-C:3771

Bread

'Give bread for the love of God and you will receive bread. Spare a life for the love of God and you will be granted life.' M1:408-C:2245

'We mistook the full moon as a loaf of bread
and raised our hands to the sky.' M1:422-C:2265

'Saturn was sighted before the creation of the heavens;
bread was sighted before grain.' M2:62-C:175

'Even if there is no bread the love of bread alone is nourishment for the lover; you cannot tie a true being to form.' M3:352-C:321

'Should you ever be nourished by that sea of light you would cast soil on bread and tandır alike.' M4:278-C:1959

'Love breathes life even into lifeless bread; it renders immortal life that is no more.' M5:327-C:2014

'Spurt like water and flood the whole world, just as the water gushed from Noah's tandır; why do you become a baker's tandır and fill yourself only with bread.' D3:311-C:3025

'My poem is like corn bread; you cannot eat it
once the night has passed.' D5:134-C:1534

'Even barley bread is haram to the body, just serving it is a pity; you place bread made from wholewheat flour before him.' M5:532-C:3489

Azık (Food to be Eaten During Journeys)

'A scholar's food is the works that sprout from his pen. And the Sufi's? Footprints.' M2:61-C:161

'Once the food of abstinence becomes your food you have become immortal; death is dead and gone.' M2:207-C:1381

'It is to spread food and drink before those who lack it that we concede such importance to the land.' M4:150-C:1006

Meals

'The fox prostrated himself during namaz; then he said: this fat cow, o elect sultan, is your mid-morning meal. And a stew can be prepared from the goat, for the blessed sultan to eat at midday. As for the rabbit: it will make a fine titbit for his kindness and beneficence the sultan in the evening.' M1:525-C:3117–9

Cuisine

'The food of those in the west comes from Andalucia, those in the east are blessed with the sustenance of Hürmüz.'[2] D1:69-C:627

'How long will the sun's heat continue as our chef? How many Jupiters will reduce the market place for the crowds?' D2:442-C:3719

'That unparalleled beauty has taken possession of my heart's kitchen with all its title deeds; and is smashing my pots, pans, plates, platters to pieces.' D4:392-C:3766

Cooking

'The sun is our chef by God's ordainment,
to call it God is foolishness.' M4:95-C:578

'Pouring water on boiling oil is fatal for both range and cauldron.'
M4:531-C:3816

'Hush, the sultan has entered the kitchen tonight and is cooking,
his face full of joy and contentment. This is unprecedented,
that sweet beloved is making our helva.' D1:33-C:264

Being Cooked

'Cook, mature and be spared the fate of spoiling.' m2:203-C:1322

'The cauldron of love that dreams of the lover who cooks and matures
raw foods has once again ascended to the brain's highest point,
and begun to boil and cook the brain.' D2:370-C:3102

'Behold Lord Şems-i from Tebriz, come to the Taurus constellation to
cook and mature me, delectably, on the tree of life.' D2:3-C:10

'In short, my whole life can be summed up with these words:
I was raw, I was cooked, I was burned.' D5:69-C:815

Food

'Through the prayers of Mary's son Jesus, food rained down from the sky to the people of Sheba.' D3:258-C:2457

'Food and words are both permitted to the mature.
You are not mature, do not eat, be as mute.' M1:334-C:1630

'You are the bounteous cloud of Moses in Desert El-Tih.
From that cloud rained exquisite, unparalleled food and loaves.'
M1:620-C:3746

'Just as the expression "the Almighty will be my host" is widespread, the words "He will fill my stomach, He will quench my thirst" describe this meal.' M1:620-C:3753

'Do not seek explanantions, accept this food, that it may be transformed into milk and honey inside you.' M1:620-C:3754

'Bodily sensations feed on darkness,
while the sensations of life are nourished by the sun.' M2:21-C:51

'The oil lamp of these sensations, its wick at its base,
is wholly dependent on sleeping, eating and drinking.'
M4:69-C:427

'The shadow of the Guide is better than naming God in vain;
a single opin- ion is better than a hundred plates of food.'
M6:553-C:3795

'While there is no life in the body there can be no pleasure in form or attire; while there is no food on the table there is no use for pots and pans.' D3:397-C:3834

Lokma[3]

'Food [lokma] that intensifies light, increases maturity, is food earned by helal means.' M1:336-C:1646

'Knowledge is born of helal food [lokma], as is wisdom; love comes out of helal food, as does compassion.' M1:336-C:1653

'Because you are at once food [lokma] and the eater of food, o my beloved, come to your senses; you are both eater and eaten.' M5:127-C:718

'O covetous soul, eat only what food [lokma] will fit in your mouth and stomach; be it helva or paluze.'[4] M5:240-C:1399

The Table

'The mature man who delivers a discourse is like a man who has laid out a feast; his table is spread with every imaginable dish. No guest goes hungry, goes without food; and there is something there to suit everytaste.' M3:222-C:1896

'God's table was laid out without purchase, or barter or the exchange of coins.' M1:54-C:80

'Christ's seat of worship is the table of the master of love …
On no account, o troubled soul, depart from this door.' M3:46-C:298

'Spreading the table, inviting guests shows, o exalted ones, that
my heart is directed towards you; this heart manifests its purity.'
M5:33-C:185

'Wondrous is the Messiah's ever-spread table;
wondrous is Mary's table, not bound to any orchard.' M6:200-C:1310

'I feed my slaves whatever I eat at my own table.' M6:594-C:3982

'Heaven above is the lid of the vessel containing worldly nutriment;
how shall I speak of its table, is it within the tongue's power?'
D1:226-C:2114

'As you are Christ, sit us at the same table as Mary,
let us eat from the same bowl; make our hearts' tambour cry out
in harmony, in the same melody as the zurna.'[5] D2:141-C:1142

'I sat down at the table of love, I tasted its bread and salt;
love became my throat, I transformed myself into lokma [food]
and swallowed myself.' D3:155-C:1359

'Be silent, read no more, this feast, this table is sufficient;
your table will sat- isfy the appetite of both Greek and Turk
until doomsday.' D4:403-C:3895

'I have covered over the earthly table; now uncork the heavenly ewer.'
D5:216-C:2503

Fasting/Ramadan

'Ho moon-faced beloved, the month of Ramadan is here.
Cover the table over and unveil the path to greatness.' D2:14-C:114

'If love were thought alone, comprised wholly of meaning, the
form of prayers and fasting would crumble away and disappear.'
M1:459-C:2636

'Emaciation from fasting pales the complexion, dizzies the mind,
but this form of emaciation, this form of pallor, are the means to
gaining the world.' D2:14-C:123

'Seal your mouth against bread, the month of fasting has come round,
like sugar. You have seen the virtues of eating and drinking,
now see the virtues of fasting.' D2:183-C:1483

'It emaciates the neck, but gives assurance in death.
A full stomach comes from eating and drinking,
and drunkenness from fasting.' D2:183-C:1491

'Ho don't fly away, fly with wings of abstinence
that a yearning to arrive has deprived of many a night's sleep,
ascend to that vault of heaven.' D2:210

'The month of Rajab[6] has come, to behold that breathtaking moon
face, to see those who are burnt and destroyed on the road,
to observe their wishes.' d2:261-c:2109

*'The month of fasting is here, the sultan's banner has arrived;
withdraw your hand from food, the table of life,
the nutriment of life is here.'* D4:336-C:3243

Bayram (Religious Festival)

'Ho, you who eat divine nutriment for sahur[7] *before fasting,
break your fast, eat a hearty meal: the crescent moon
of bayram has appeared.'* D2-C:352

'The month of fasting has passed, bayram is here. The night of separation has passed, the beloved has been sighted, has suddenly appeared.' D2:44-C:354

*'Bayram is here, bayram is here, that blessed good fortune is here;
take up the drum and play, for that moon has shown her face.'*
D2:51-C:408

'Bayram has arrived, how wretched were we in its absence, let us unite with bayram now, for that food-laden table, that tirit[8] *has arrived.'*
D2:51-C:413

'O Bayram, lay the table and be avenged on Ramadan, establish a new order, with that cascading, curling, jet-black hair, reunite and bring us together once again.' D2:172-C:1387

*'O Lord Şems-i from Tebriz, you are both patience and abstinence;
at once bayram scattering sugar, and the glory,
majesty and might of fasting.'* D2:183-C:1495

'This is the sufis' bayram, it is familiar with these serving trays; but even without trays what would bayram be lacking? Bayram would still be bayram.' D2:289-C:2367

'The blessedness of the Night of Power,[9] the month of fasting, the day of bayram, the blessedness of the union of Adam and Eve.' D3:89-C:674

'Koruk[10] matured and was liberated from unripeness; when it matures it turns sweet; when the fasting month ends, it's bayram.' D3:158-C:1388

Kurban Bayram (The Feast of the Sacrifice)

'The man slaughtered a lamb, gave out loaves; for the moon he had been awaiting had appeared out of gold dust.' M6:108-C:601

The Mevlit Kandil[11]

I did not come across any couplets related to the Mevlit Kandil.

The Berat Kandil[12]

'The day of Berat is here, renew the lover's title of privilege. The time for zakah[13] is upon us, donate your ruby lips in zakah.' D3:111-C:900

The Miraç Kandil[14]

'If you stand in the line of those destined for the miraç it will take you on its back like an oblivious Burak[15] and raise you up to the heavens.'
M4:88-C:552

The Night of Power

'Tonight your face was born like a full moon, the Night of Power has arrived; o sultan of all beauties, I beg you, do not sleep tonight.'
D2:30-C:245

'Tonight is as though it were the Night of Power, be silent and serve, thus may each of God's souls attain God's admiration.' D2:49-C:396

Aşure Day[16] (The Tenth Day of Muharram[17])

'On the day of aşure the Shi'a weeps for the Karbala incident,18 crying out for help.' M6:135-C:3782

Couplets Mentioning the Food Groups

PROTEINS

Meat

'Like the Turks' meat dishes this tale I have told is half cooked;
hear the complete version from Hakim-i Gaznevi.' M3:446-C:3750

'How many cows and sheep have you eaten,
how many camels have you sacrificed.' M4:316-C:2246

Offal

'Today that friend who is partial to liver said,
"I will be your guest tonight."

Thread the liver on to the skewers, o heart,
prepare kebab for the guest.' D5:458-C:6249

'I don't eat sheep's head, it's indigestible; nor sheep's trotters either,
they're nothing but bone.' D5:233-C:2695

Fish

'The water advanced to fish is its bread and its water,
its clothing, its medicine and its sleep.' M6:607-C:4058

Eggs

'The egg is now empty of the bird,
but you have hatched from the egg of life.' D:404-C:3259

'A young philosopher who believed in nature thought the sky looked like an egg and the earth like its yolk.' M1:445-C:2472

'You may be certain that faith with blasphemy is like the white and yolk of this egg; there is a barzakh19 separating them, they do not mix.' D4:74-C:640

Poultry and Game

'The falcon too brings prey from the hills; but gliding with its own wings it is hunted; the sultan therefore keeps it with the partridge and the hazel grouse.' M6:700-C:4678

Pulses

'My stone is the size of a chick pea, but come wartime
it spares neither head nor helmet.' M2:88-C:350

'That universe resembles a mill, while this one is like a threshing field; here, are you wheat or bean? Be what you are, you will be the same there too.' D1:11-C:54

Nuts

'O trustworthy man, the world has rotted, it is a hollow walnut; do not attempt to test it, observe it from a distance.' M6:511-C:3478

'For example, when you give children who have been playing with walnuts shelled walnuts or walnut oil, they won't take them.' FM:128

'Children are bribed with walnuts and currants; were we not children, would we be worthy of walnuts and grapes?' D2:380-C:3177

'O carnal hazelnut, know your friend to be love; it seeks your life, requests it, and thus penetrates your shell.' M5:315-C:1932

MILK

Milk Products

'Those at the stage of growth and development drink milk; those dependent on feet wear rawhide sandals.' M2:274-C:1734

'This speech is milk in life's breast; if not sucked by a beautiful being, it will not flow.' M4:435-C:2387

'O Moses' mother, give him milk, suckle him; cast him into the water, fear not that he will come to harm.' M2:420-C:2973

'On earth they are as Moses and Harun. They blend into one another like milk and honey, and become one.' M4:532-C:3831

'God provided milk for the nourishment of children; He made every woman's breasts into milk taps.' M5:274-C:1634

'The goats were home for milking by dinnertime.' M5:23-C:77

'What harm does it do the camel's milk if the milker smashes a pot?' D5:353-C:4473

Cheese

'I resemble milk in terms of taste, I do not stick in the throat; be not misguided and regard me as salty like cheese, do not judge incorrectly.' D1:288-C:2671

Yogurt

'Pharaoh sank into the water like yogurt and drowned; while Moses floated on the surface, like oil.' D1:311-C:2884

'You are still that sour ayran[20] *in the pot; you have still not managed to skim the fat off that yogurt.'* M6:276-C:1789

FRUIT AND VEGETABLES

Fruit

'Fruit is meaning; while flowers are the form of the meaning. That flower is good news; while fruit is its nutriment.' M1:488-C:2942

'O great ones, this world is like a tree; and we are as half ripe fruit hanging from its branches.' M3:171-C:1295

'The soul inclines towards wisdom and knowledge; while the body inclines towards vineyards, gardens, greenery, grapes.' M3:505-C:4439

'Think of the heavens and the earth as an apple grown on God's omnipotent tree.' M4:267-C:1869

'The tree that drinks apple juice sprouts apple leaves; that which drinks date juice will yield dates.' D5:389-C:5132

'Iblis said "It is beautiful" but he said it with a scowl, pursing his lips like a squeezed Seville orange.' M5:166-C:944

'The fire in Mary's heart turned the branch with parched lips into a blessed palm sapling.' M6:198-C:1293

'Sweet fruit is concealed on the branch, under the leaf; immortal life is con- cealed in death.' M6:531-C:3583

'Upon beholding Yusuf 's face once again, the virtuous women of Egypt each seized a Seville orange and began slashing their hands.'
D2:370-C:3098

'You are just a parched palm sapling in the eyes of the Jew, and yet, to soothe Mary's troubles, you yield hundreds of fresh dates.'
D2:456-C:3878

'Why are the branches of the peach tree short and low?
So it can yield its peaches to the plucker, is that not so, I said.'
D4:72-C:601

'"Why such a pale face?" the pomegranate kept asking of the quince; the quince replied: "The pearls you keep hidden inside you have paled and faded me."' D4:72-C:605

'The branch keeps a tight grip on unripe fruit.' D5:363-C:4680

'One day Luqman's21 master received a water melon as a gift; he bid someone thus: 'My son, go and fetch Luqman.'
M2:232-C:1514

'To the lover nourished on divine love, hundreds of bodies have not the worth of a single mulberry leaf.' M5:424-C:2717

'My grapes are ripe, why stoop to squeezing verjuice?'
I:112-C:1043

'There are fine satins in mulberry leaves.'
D:389-C:3087

Vegetables

'Eventually, out of base ingratitude, they demanded leeks, cress and lettuce.' M1:620-C:3751

'Be it onions or garlic, every plant in the garden has its own furrow.' M4:157-C:1083

'If a man took a single radish from a shop and a wise man said, "It is God's will," you would say, "Put it back where you found it" and, thumping his head, add, "This too is God's will."'
M5:471-C:3061–2

'To a cucumber field, a cabbage field, an onion field, or to a rose garden?' FM:169

'Think of me as spinach and prepare me as you will; sour or sweet, cooked means reunion with you, oneness with you.'
D2:123-C:997

'It is no surprise if an unbeliever is sour, aubergines have a rapport with sourness.' D:4209-B:1955

'I am like sugar, like honey; yet you command me to be sour. Transform cowpeas into beans if you are able.' D:332

'What does anyone who eats opium poppy pods with lettuce care for the kiss or the embrace; do you suppose that grieves them?'
MEK:35

'Is pedestrian a word worth uttering? Even in sleep he advances, like Ashabi Kehf;[22] *they lay on their sides too, but got all the way to heaven. The pumpkin joined their gathering; it arrived, erected its pole and climbed up the string. How did it see, how did it know, how did it learn how to do it? It knew from the giver of that rambling, stretching, rising string, it learned from Him.'* D:4:73-C:613–4

'Do not crawl into a turnip furrow and open your mouth; the turnip cannot accompany you in wit or on journeys.' M4:157-C:1087

FLOWERS

'Do not eat barley like donkeys, but rather redbud in Huten.'[23] M5:389-C:2475

Accustom your stomach to sweet basil and roses, that the prophets' wisdom may be yours, eat of their nutriment.' M5:390-C:2477

PLANTS

'The hazelnut and the opium poppy have come to the plain, mint and cress to the banks of the spring.' D5:53-C:632

'O, says black death; whatever plants, medicinal weeds, leaves and meadow grass you have eaten, give them back.' M1:359-C:1903

'Were I to offer you my heart, my life, still it would be like taking cress to Kirman.' M1:534-C:3207

'I called Satan by the name of Gabriel; and blatantly referred to cardoon as a guiding light.' D5:170-C:1936

GRAIN

'He who sows crops ends up with an empty granary, but he reaps the benefits in the field.' M1:408-C:2248

Wheat-Flour

'Like a fine sieve separating flour from husk, the trials on this fearful road sift out the brave from the fainthearted.' M6:90-C:13

'The ant worships a single grain of wheat because it does not see the threshing field.' M6:137-C:512

'He converts sand into flour for Halil[24] *and converts the hills and stones into friends for Davut.'* M6:350-C:2289

'Every one of these roads leads to the same house; these thousands of ears of corn are from a single seed.' M6:543-C:3679

Bulgur

'He raised his hand to strike the head of the sufi who worshipped bulgur aş.'[25] M6:202-C:1334

Rice

'These lentils are the rice of the cross-eyed;
because there is no rice, nor lentils here.' D5:293-C:3483

Fat, Sugar and Others

LIPIDS

Butter

'If you have fresh ayran that has not been skimmed, do not drink it without churning and collecting the cream.' M4:426-C:3048

'Where is the one who merged with me like milk with honey; where is the one who, like water and oil, will not be reconciled with me?' d2:455-c:3862 'Like oil that blends into milk-like life, the world of no abode arrives at the world of home.' D4:286-C:2767

Olive Oil

'And that is why you ask repeatedly why do you do this in this way; because form is olive oil, and meaning light.' M4:418-C:2994

'The entire household was struck with wonder to behold how that single drop of olive oil had filled this oil lamp.' M5:42-C:380

'A lamp without wick or olive oil can shine neither brightly nor dimly.' M6:658-C:4438

'The soul is olive oil, enamoured of fire; it seeks fire as the lover seeks the beloved.' D4:149-C:1338

Sesame Oil

'It gives not the slightest thought to drawing water or extracting oil from sesame seeds.' M6:342-C:2200

If the donkey eats all the sesame seeds, where will we extract the oil for the lamp?' D5:153-C:1766

Suet

'Without being a scientist you cannot transform suet into clarified fat; but take a look at the one who gives the eye, composed of suet, the ability to see, and compare His knowledge.' D2:63-C:519

SWEETENERS

Honey

'Do not sell vinegar and you will see thousands of souls immersed by their faith in a sea of honey.' M1:434-C:2384

'The beauty of milk and honey becomes manifest when lit up by the rays of the heart; the beauty of every thing of beauty stems from the heart.' M3:252-C:2266

'The ayah [verse] "God gave divine inspiration to the honey bee" arrived and, touched by divine inspiration, the honey bee's house filled with sweetness.' M5:208-C:1229

'He transformed the honey bee into thick cream inside, to serve as medicine for the sick.' M5:274-C:1630

'On hills, in hives, on trees, honey bees fill depots of sugared honey.' M6:8-C:34

'Our bodies are like a beehive and the wax and honey in the hive are God's love. Mothers and fathers are bees. Occasionally as His vehicle they are disciplined by the gardener. It is the gardener who makes the hive.' FM:335

'May they harmonise with one another, like milk and honey; become part of each other, like sugar and helva, be faithful, become one.' D3:89-C:677

'Once the pleasure of faith has blossomed in your heart,
how can worldly honey ever seem tasty?' D5:139-C:1594

'Your sweetness also testifies that you were raised on honey
at the Elest meclis.'[26] D4:298-C:2886

Pekmez (grape syrup)

'Just then it occurred to that poor soul to say, stop this nonsense; vinegar is pekmez, and pekmez is vinegar.' M6:473-C:3191

Sugar

'If they fed me all the poison in the world
I would convert it to sugar inside me.' D5:303-C:3629

'Noah's community poured vinegar over his summons.
But the sea of kindness poured sugar over Noah.' M6:7-C:20

'If you wish him to be as sugar to you,
gaze upon him through the eyes of a lover.' M4:19-C:74

'My soul consumed the sugar of love in such quantities in Egypt
that my cries made sugar blossom in the heart of my reed flute.'
D1:327-C:3007

'There is sugar concealed in the breath blowing into the reed flute, the flute resembling Mary fell pregnant to breath far sweeter.' D2:14-C:120

'O shopkeeper, sugar has arrived from Egypt; Yusuf, as sweet as sugar, has suddenly arrived from his travels.' D2:62-C:503

'What is better my friend, sugar or the maker of sugar? My friend, is the moon or the moon's creator more beautiful?' D2:63-C:514

'At this moment the love birds are spreading their wings, because kantars of sugar are on their way from Egypt.' D2:348-C:2903

'What need for Egypt's sugar cane? When Şems-i Tebrizi's words, laden with sugar, are hundreds of sugar cane.' D3:191-C:1753

'Ask for sweet akide[27] *in the garden of love, because nature sells only vinegar and squeezes verjuice.'* D3:326-C:3195

'I pour rivers of sugar into the narrow soul of sugar cane;
I bring noble, joyful thoughts to mind.' D1 (CLXIII)

Spices

'Laughter, reunion, coming together smell of saffron,
while tears and distance have the stench of onions.' M6:606-C:4053

'How can I not laugh, how can I conceal my laughter? I am a laughing pomegranate; a sugar cane, sugar is not, after all, going to behave as sumach.' D3:333-C:3270

'Speak not of musk; your breath carries the stench of onions, disclosing what you withhold.' M4:246-C:1775

'Because this is like taking cumin to Kirman.'[28] MEK:82

'There is joy in the soul-enlightening assembly again; arise, cast black cumin seed into the fire, to ward off the evil eye.' M6:158-C:948

'May your arrival be preserved from the evil eye, let us cast harmal and black cumin seeds into the fire; but what is harmal seed, and what is black cumin seed? Like the agalloch tree, let us cast ourselves into the fire and burn ourselves.' D3:119-C:999

'They show a handful of something, like a handful of pepper [black pepper], a handful of mastic chewing gum from every storehouse.' FM:96

'Like someone dying of thirst he circled the edge of the pool, searching for water; suddenly, like dried mint he fell into my pool, was soaked, and became a companion for my bread.' DI (CLXII)-C:3590

'Purge yourself of denying the beloved, that the perfume of sweet basil from the beloved's rose garden may reach your heart.' M4:87-C:550

'That pen, he said, wrote astounding words; it transformed the page into a field of sweet basil, an iris field, a rose garden.' M4:519-C:3722

'Be it good or evil, be it no bigger than a mustard seed, be it inside a stone, up in the heavens, or down here on earth, still God will bring it out into the open.' MEK:157

Appetisers

'Cook appetisers from tears on thy heart's fire; field and flower have been debauched by the clouds and sun.' M1:336-C:1646

'If there is no joy in your heart, if you are unworthy of the wine cup, and do not care for wine, what can I do? What does a child intoxicated by roasted chick peas grasp from his lips, what does he hear?' D3:25-C:162

'The almond inside the nut is pure and beautiful, the outside shell, skin; in- side the shell it becomes ripe and pure, just like a chicken's egg.' D4:73-C:620

'You are aware of how lovely the date is outside, while inside it is all stone? Well, man of compassion, be the opposite, like the fig be beautiful inside as well as out.' D4:73-C:621

'O elevated soul, you were fire, you became divine light; you were koruk,[29] *you became grapes and now you have become as a sultana.'* M4:472-C:3421

'When you wish to be certain, you find your mosque cluttered with carob beans.' M4:55-C:387

Vinegar

'As vinegar becomes more acid, sugar must grow sweeter.' M6:7-C:17

'Tribulation is vinegar. And kindness is like honey; the two form the basis of sirkencübin.'[30] M6:7-C:18

A Guide to Turkish Pronunciation

Turkish is pronounced exactly as it looks on the page. There are 29 letters in the Turkish alphabet, made up of eight vowels and 21 consonants. Most are pronounced in the same way as English, with the following exceptions:

A – pronounced as the *u* in umbrella
C – pronounced as the *j* in job
Ç – pronounced as the *ch* in chair
E – pronounced only as the *e* in end
G – pronounced only as the *g* in garden
Ğ – a soft sound, similar to a *w*, which lengthens a preceding vowel
I – without a dot, pronounced as the unstressed *er* sound in English in words like hamburger, teacher, etc
J – pronounced as the *s* in pleasure
O – pronounced only as the *o* in orange
Ö – pronounced as the *ur* in words like hurt, curt, etc
Ş – pronounced as the *sh* in shop
U – pronounced as the *oo* in cook
Ü – pronounced as the ü in German or the French *tu*

Glossary of Terms

Bıçak Arası – literally 'between knives,' a way of chopping meat very finely, using two knives placed side by side, the blades touching each other. Using one hand to hold the handles and the other to guide the blades, chop the diced meat as finely as possible, until it resembles, but is not quite the same as, minced meat.

Börek – pastries stuffed with meat, cheese, etc, then fried or baked.

Caul Fat – lacy, fatty membrane encasing the internal organs of an animal. Used in Turkish cuisine for wrapping köfte, etc.

Çile (Chille) – a 40-day trial period of fasting and spiritual retreat. For disciples of the Mevlevi Order the çile usually consisted of 1001 days of service in the kitchen.

Clarified Butter – ordinary butter that has been treated to remove any non-fat elements in order to improve it as a cooking medium. Clarified butter can be heated to higher temperatures than regular butter. To clarify butter melt gently until the butter begins to separate, forming a thick layer in the pan. Most of the milk solids will drop to the bottom of the pan and a layer of white foam will form on top. Remove the pan from the heat so as not to disturb the layers, spoon off the top layer of foam and pour the pure butter into a container. Discard the milky residue from the bottom of the pan. Clarified butter keeps for several weeks in the refrigerator. Clarified butter can be bought from Indian shops and some supermarkets.

Çömlek – an earthenware pot sculpted from clay.

Dergah – a dervish lodge, usually a humble building. However dergahs with sufficient funding contained not only cells for the dervishes to live in, but also a kitchen and a mosque. It is also called a tekke.

Fat-Tailed Sheep – the fat is used for cooking. See page 46 for alternatives.

Gold Vark – edible, gossamer-thin sheets of pure gold, used to decorate food, sold sandwiched between two sheets of paper, available in Indian groceries and cake-decorating shops. Vark sheets are so fragile that they dissolve easily when touched, which is why it's best to remove the top piece of paper from a sheet of vark and then invert it on top of the food that is to be decorated. It will keep indefinitely, untarnished, if stored in an airtight container.

Halife Dede – a disciple who has been appointed by a spiritual guide to be his chief successor.

Helal (Halal) – in Islamic law, something that is permissible, legitimate.

Hu – an Islamic term, meaning there is no God but He. For Sufis it refers to the essence of God. Hu-Allah has 1001 names, 99 of which are mentioned in the Holy Koran and the Sacred Hadith as Esmaü'l Hüsna (the most beautiful names). Hu, commonly used in Tasavvuf, particularly by the Mevlevi order, is the shortest of Allah's names.

Koruk – unripe grape.

Madrasah, Madrasa – a theological school attached to a mosque for the training of spiritual leaders.

Mastic Gum – derived from the resin of the mastic tree and softened with beeswax. Transparent yellow in colour, it is used crushed with salt in Turkish cuisine to flavour desserts and meat dishes. Available in Turkish groceries.

Meydan – the room where devotional ceremonies take place, and where new dervishes are taught to whirl for the sema, sing hymns or recite Mevlana's poetry.

Muhib – a lover or patron of a Sufi master or order, someone affiliated. In the Mevlevi tradition it is the entry level of a beginner who has had the first initiation.

Murshid – 'one who guides'. The Sufi master and spiritual guide of a Sufi disciple.

Niyaz – the neediness of a dervish before God. Because God responds to genuine need, the dervish must become more needy in order to receive divine blessings and become nearer to God. Niyaz is also the humble manner in which a Sufi greets his superior.

Pekmez – grape molasses, available in Turkish groceries.

Pomegranate Juice – yellow, sour pomegranates are difficult to obtain in Britain, but Middle Eastern groceries sell pomegranate syrup, also called pomegranate molasses, made from the juice of the sour variety cooked down with a little sugar. In recipes calling for sour pomegranate juice, dilute 1 tablespoon of pomegranate syrup in 250 ml (1 cup) of warm water. Alternatively you can use sweet pomegranate juice, soured with 1 tablespoon of strained fresh lemon (or lime) juice, per cup of pomegranate juice.

Saç – iron utensil, like a shallow wok, used for frying börek, etc.

Sema – whirling dance performed by the Mevlevi dervishes.

Sohbet – the company, speech and conversation of a spiritual master. In Sufism, sohbet is believed to be a primary means of transmission of the grace of the spiritual master.

Sumach – (*rhus coriaria*) the sour berries of a wild shrub. Fresh berries are steeped in water, and the sour water is used in cooking. Deep burgundy in colour, they can also be dried and ground to use as a spice to give dishes a sour flavour. Available in Turkish groceries.

Tandır – a clay oven sunk into a pit in the ground.

Tariqat – the Sufi path of spiritual purification and training in mystical disciplines.

Tarikatçı Dede – the chief spiritual guide of the Mevlevis, who assisted the Çelebi of the order, the chief authority of the order.

Tasavvuf – the mystical dimension of Islam. The mystical science of spiritual purification and seeking oneness with God.

Verjuice – the sour juice of green or unripe grapes.

Wild Radish Leaves – also called Jointed Charlock (species *raphanus aphanistrum*). A winter annual with hairy, lobed leaves, belonging to the mustard family. Found in North America.

Taster Panellists

My tasters (panellists) were:

Tülin Arıcılar	*Retired teacher*
Ülkü Arıcılar	*Housewife*
Şaziye Arısoy	*Cookery teacher*
Handan Aygın	*Housewife*
Dr Nilgün Çelebi	*University lecturer*
Nimet Çetinkaya	*Cookery teacher*
Dr Nermin Işık	*Assistant associate professor*
Hasan Halıcı	*Mechanical engineer*
Nermin Halıcı	*Housewife*
Filiz Yalçıner	*Architect*
Mücella Yalçıner	*Cookery teacher*

Notes

Recipes from Mevlana's Works

1. Place where the souls of the dead await the day of judgement (located between the world and hell).
2. Stringed instrument made with a coconut shell.
3. Meat and vegetable soup served with dumplings.
4. The prophet Muhammed's uncle.
5. See Bulamaç, p. 44.
6. The last (optional) prayer before dawn.
7. Sun-dried spicy beef with garlic.

Selected Couplets from Mevlana's Works Related to Food and Drink

1. Prayer recited on certain occasions by a muezzin before he recites the call to prayer.
2. Hürmüz belonged to the Iranian royal family and received a letter from the Holy Prophet Muhammed inviting him to embrace Islam. Although he did not respond at first he later converted.
3. As well as being a fried, syrup-filled dumpling, lokma is the generic term for food used by Mevlevi Sufis.
4. See Palüze, p. 131.
5. A reed instrument resembling an oboe, played at weddings together with the davul (drums) to announce the arrival of the bride.
6. The seventh month of the Muslim calendar, one of the three

holy months, along with Sha'ban and Ramadan, when God answers all prayers.

7. Meal eaten just before dawn during Ramadan.
8. See Tirit, p. 140.
9. The twenty-seventh night of Ramadan, when the Koran was revealed.
10. See Glossary, Koruk.
11. The religious celebration held on the evening of the Prophet Muhammed's birth.
12. The Night of Pardon, the night between the 14th and the 15th days of the month Sha'ban, the eighth month of the lunar year in the Islamic calendar and the month immediately preceding Ramadan.
13. Distribution of 1/40 of one's income as alms.
14. The annual celebration commemorating the Miraç (Muhammed's ascent to heaven).
15. Burak was the name of the winged horse Muhammed rode during his ascent to heaven. It literally means 'White Horse' but is also translated as Thunder- Lightning.
16. See Aşure, p. 129.
17. The first month of the Muslim calendar.
18. The massacre of the Prophet Muhammed's grandson Imam Hüseyin, together with 72 of his friends.
19. Place where the souls of the dead await the day of judgement (located between the world and hell). Interspace between life on earth and life in the hereafter.
20. See Ayran, p. 145.
21. A black slave, the most celebrated sage of the East, famous for his fables and proverbs.
22. Ashabi Kehf was put to sleep in a cave for 309 years in order

to save him from his persecutors and ensure his resurrection after death.

23. A town on the banks of an agricultural stream, 300km southeast of Yarkent, Turkistan, known for its natural beauty.
24. The exceedingly generous prophet Halil.
25. See Bulgur Aş, p. 79.
26. The assembly at which God asks his souls, before he has enterd their body, if they accept Him as their God.
27. Hard candy made with sugary syrup flavoured with bergamot, orange, lemons, mint or nuts.
28. Persian city where cumin is very plentiful.
29. Unripe grapes.
30. See Sirkencübin, p. 49.

Bibliography

Books

Ali Eşref Dede, *Yemek Risalesi* (*Food Treatise*), adapted by Feyzi Halıcı, Ankara, Atatürk Kültür Merkezi, 1992.

Baytop, Turhan, *Türkiye'de Bitkilerle Tedavi* (Healing with Plants in Turkey), Istanbul, 1984, pp. 392–3.

Can, Şefik, *Mevlana, Hayatı,* Şahsiyeti, *Fikirleri* (*Mevlana, His Life, Personality and Ideas*), Istanbul, Ötüken Yayınları, 1995.

Eflaki, Ahmet, *Ariflerin Menkibleri 1* (*The Book of the Wise 1*), Fourth Edition, Istanbul, Remzi Kitabevi, 1986.

Eflaki, Ahmet, *Ariflerin Menkibeleri 2*, (*The Book of the Wise 2*), Fourth Edition, Istanbul, Remzi Kitabevi, 1987.

Es, Selçuk, *Konya Yemekleri*, (*Food from Konya*) Konya, Yıldız Basımevi, 1965. Gölpınarlı, Abdülbaki, *Mevlana'dan Sonra Mevlevilik*, (*The Mevlevi Order After Mevlana*), Second Edition, Istanbul, Inkilap ve Aka Kitabevleri, 1983.

Halıcı, Feyzi, Mevlana Celaleddin Hayatı Ve Eserleri (Mevlana Celaleddin, His Life and His Works) Konya, Publisher: Doğuş Ofset Matbaa, 1983.

Halıcı, Nevin, *Geleneksel Konya Yemekleri*, (*Traditional Dishes from Konya*), Ankara, Güven Matbaası, 1979.

Halıcı, Nevin, *Ege Bölgesi Yemekleri* (*Dishes from the Aegean Region*) Ankara, Güven Matbaası, 1981.

Halıcı, Nevin, *Akdeniz Bölgesi Yemekleri* (*Mediterranean Food*), Konya, Arı Basımevi, 1983.

Halıcı, Nevin, *Nevin Halıcı's Turkish Cookbook*, London, Dorling Kindersley Limited, 1989.

Halıcı, Nevin, *Güneydoğu Anadolu Bölgesi Yemekleri* (*Dishes From Southeast Anatolia*), Konya, Arı Ofset Matbaacılık, 1983.

Halıcı, Nevin, 'A Kitchen in Sille,' *The Cook's Room*, London, MacDonalds Illustrated Books, 1991.

Halıcı, Nevin, *Konya'da Kışlık Yiyecekler Üzerine Bir Araştırma* (*A Study of Winter Fare in Konya*), Ankara, Güray Ofset Matbaacılık, 2000.

Halıcı, Nevin, *Dishes from the Black Sea*, Ankara, Güray Ofset Matbaacılık, 2001. Helou, Anissa, *Mediterranean Street Food,* New York, Harper Collins, 2002.

Kamil Mehmet, *Melceü't Tabbahin*, Istanbul, Şeyh Yahya Matbaası, 1990.

Konya 1973 Provincial Annual.

Koşay, Z, Hamit and Ülkücan Akile, *Anadolu Yemekleri ve Türk Mutfağı* (*Anatolian food and Turkish Cuisine*), Ankara, M.E.B., 1965.

Mevlana, Celaleddin, *Mektuplar* (*Letters*), translated by A. Gölpınarlı, İnkılap ve Aka Kitabevleri, 1963.

Mevlana Celaleddin, *Mecalis-i Saba*, translated by A. Gölpınarlı, Konya, Yeni Kitap Basımevi, 1965.

Mevlana, *Divan*, Translated by A. Gölpınarlı, Istanbul, Milliyet

Yayınları, 1971. Mevlana Celaleddin, *Divan-ı Kebir, I, II, III, IV, V*, adapted by A. Gölpınarlı,

Istanbul, Remzi Kitabevi, 1957–60.

Mevlana, *Mesnevi ve* Şerhi (*Mesnevi and* Şerhi), *I, II, III, IV, V, VI,* commentary by Abdülbaki Gölpınarlı, second edition, Istanbul, M.E.B., 1985.

Mevlana, *Fihi Mafih,* translated by M.Ü. Kahya, Istanbul, M.E.B., 1985. Meyerovitch, Eva Ce Vitray, *Konya, Hazreti Mevlana and the Sema*, third edition,

Konya, İl Kültür Müdürlüğü Yayını, 2000.

Önder, Mehmet, *Mevlana, Mevlevilik ve Mevlana Müzesi* (*Mevlana, the Mevlevi Order and the Mevlana Museum*), Ankara, Dönmez Ofset, undated.

Sultan Veled, İbtida-Name, translated by A. Gölpınarlı, Konya Turizm Derneği Yayını, 1976.

Tebrizi, Şems-i, *Makalat 1* (*Conversations*), translated by M.N. Gençosman, Istanbul, Dizerkonca Basımevi, 1974.

Türk Dil Kurumu (Turkish Language Association), *Divanü Lügat-it Türk Dizini*, (*Official Turkish Dictionary*), Ankara, Ankara Üniversitesi Basımevi, 1972.

Yusuf Has Hacip, *Kutadgu Bilig,* second edition, translated by Raşit Rahmeti Arat, Türk Tarih Kurumu Yayını, 1998.

Yeğen, E.M., *Tatlı-Pasta Öğretimi* (*On Sweets and Cakes*), 11th edition, Istanbul, Inkilap Ve Aka Basımevi, 1977.

Articles

Cunbur, Müjgan, 'Mevlana'nın Mesnevisi'nde Ve Divan-ı Kebir'inde Yemekler' ('Food in Mevlana's Mesnevi and Divan-ı Kebir'), *Papers from the Symposium on Turkish Cuisine*, Ankara, A.Ü.B., 1982.

Cunbur, Müjgan, 'Mevlana'nın Şiirlerinde: Ekinden Ekmeğe' ('Mevlana's Poetry: From Planted Grain to Bread'), Second National Mevlana Congress (Communications), Selçuk Üniversitesi Yayınları, Konya, 1987.

Çelebi, Celaleddin, 'Uluslararası Yemek Kongresi' ('International Food Congress'), First International Food Congress, organiser: Feyzi Halıcı. Kültür ve Turizm Bakanlığı Yayını, 1988.

Davidson, Alan, 'The Seven Wonders of Konya', *Petit Propos Culinaires Magazine*, no. 24, 1986.

Gould, Kevin, 'Ten of the Best Gourmet Destinations', *Waitrose Food Illustrated Magazine*, January 2003.

Demirci, Ibrahim, 'Yüzüncü ad Romanında Konya', ('Konya in the Novel "The Hundredth Name"), *Konya Magazine*, no. 28, p. 32, 2001.

Halıcı, Feyzi, 'Neolitik Çağdan Günümüze Türk Mutfağı ve bu Mutfağın Kutsal İnancımızdaki Yeri' ('Turkish Cuisine from the Neolithic Age to Today and its Place in our Religious Beliefs'), *Papers from the Symposium on Turkish Cuisine,* Ankara, A.Ü.B. 1982.

Halıcı, Nevin, 'Konya'da Özel Gün Yemekleri' ('Special Occasion Food in Konya'), *Türk Halk Edebiyatı ve Folklorunda Yeni Görüşler I* (*New Views of Turkish Folk Literature and Folklore*), adapted by Feyzi

Halıcı, Konya Kültür ve Turizm Derneği Yayını, Ankara, 1985.

Halıcı, Nevin, 'Geçmişte ve Günümüzde Konya Pilavı' ('Konya Pilav Past and Present'), *Yeni Gazete*, Konya, 23 March 1999.

Halıcı, Nevin, 'Mevlana'nın Kullandığı Yemek Sembolleri' ('Food Symbols Used by Mevlana'), International Food Festival, Izmir, 2002, unpublished.

Melikof, Irene, 'Le rituel de Helva: recherches sur une coutume des corporations de métiers dans la Turquie mediévale', *Islam*, 1964, p. 39.

Oral, M Zeki, 'Selçuk Devri Yemekleri' ('Food in the Seljuk Era'), *Turkish Ethnography Journal*, nos 1 and 2, 1956, p. 73.

Önder, Mehmet, 'Konya'da Tarih Boyunca Helvacılık' ('Helva Making in Konya throughout History'), *Journal of Research Into Turkish Folklore*, no. 10, 1950, p. 159.

Yusufoğlu, Mehmet, 'Selçuklu Yemeklerinden Herise ve Tutmaç' ('Herise and Tutmaç from Seljuk Food'), *Anıt Magazine*, no. 16, 1950, p. 9.

Yusufoğlu, Mehmet, 'Selçuklu Devri Ekmek Adları Bazlama Bazlamaç' ('Bread Names in the Seljuk Era, Bazlama Bazlamaç'), *Turkish Ethnography Journal*, no. 1, 1956, p. 76.

In addition to the references I have quoted directly in the text, this bibliography includes other sources I found relevant, although I have not quoted from them.

I consulted my sources in three stages. In 1979, while writing my book *Traditional Dishes From Konya*, I devised a questionnaire for the first 25 people. I met the second group in 1984 for *Food for Special Occasions and Entertaining*, and the third group in 2002.

Names of Sources

GROUP I

	Name	*Age*	*District*
31.	Saadet Ongun	71	Köprübaşı
32.	Hafize Ayvacı	65	Uluırmak
33.	Fatma Zeytin	67	Türbeönü
34.	Muhlise Özücan	58	Küllükbaşı
35.	Ayşe Tırıs	75	Tahtatepen
36.	Nesibe Çalışır	78	Sedirler
37.	Sare Obalar	55	Şems Mahallesi
38.	Havva Erkoç	67	Araplar
39.	Sabriye Erkoç	75	Araplar
40.	Fatma Atanur	74	Küçük Kumköprü
41.	Fatma Balak	70	Çimenlik
42.	Sıdıka Sakal	72	Topraklık
43.	Aliye Öztermiyeci	64	Sarıyakup
44.	Hatice Nemli	60	Musalla
45.	Hacer Uslu	65	Kovanağzı
46.	Şerife Düvel	60	Mengene
47.	Sare Düvel	65	Mengene
48.	Ayşe Midiliç	90	Meram
49.	Celile Şeker	50	Gazialemşah
50.	Havva Beton	85	Lalebahçe
51.	Hanım Halıcı	73	Çifte Merdiven

52.	Kadriye Parlak	70	Postane Arkası
53.	Refika Tüfekçi	59	Türbeönü
54.	Rahime Dere	52	Havzan
55.	Emin Obalar	64	İnce Minare

GROUP 2

1.	Ayşe Cıvıl	77	Türbeönü
2.	Süreyya Ediren	80	Meram
3.	Huriye Koçbeker	59	Çukur Mektep
4.	Muhlise Özücan	63	Küllükbaşı
5.	Lütfiye Gündoğdu	62	Türbe Önü
6.	Celile Şeker	55	Köprübaşı
7.	Mediha Uluışık	70	Meram
8.	Rabia Özbakar	65	Çaybaşı
9.	Şerife Düvel	65	Mengene
10.	Fatma Atanur	79	Küçük Kumköprü
11.	Fatma Balak	74	Çimenlik

GROUP 3

12.	1. Aysel İşbilen	61	Çifte Merdiven
13.	2. Güzide Özbilgeç	61	Çifte Merdiven
14.	3. Tülin Arıcılar	55	Kazım Karabekir
15.	4. Ülkü Arıcılar	56	Kazım Karabekir
16.	5. Nermin Takurlu	72	Çifte Merdiven
17.	6. Şengül Ertuğrul	46	Kazım Karabekir

Index